DEVO
A BIOGRAPHY

RUST BELT ROCK
FROM AKRON

NICK THOMAS

GEM EDITIONS

Copyright © 2023 by GEM Editions

All rights reserved. No portion of this book may be reproduced, copied or electronically stored, by any means or technique, without the express written consent of the publisher.

ISBN: 978-1735152387

Library of Congress Cataloging-in-Publication Data

Thomas, Nick
    Devo: A Biography – Rust Belt Rock from Akron
    Includes bibliographical references
    ISBN 978-1735152387

    1. Rock music – Ohio. 2. Rock music – History and criticism. 3. Rock music – Bio-bibliography.
    I. Title

Please contact the publisher to report any errors or omissions. Organizations and other groups interested in purchasing quantities of this book should contact the publisher.

This is not an official or authorized work. Devo, their record companies, their managers and their representatives did not participate in the writing, editing, production or publication of this book.

Cover photo credit: DMI/The LIFE Picture Collection

Printed in the U.S.A.

▶ TABLE OF CONTENTS

INTRODUCTION 1
CHAPTER 1: MARK MOTHERSBAUGH 11
CHAPTER 2: JERRY CASALE 19
CHAPTER 3: KENT STATE 23
CHAPTER 4: DEVO'S DEBUT 29
CHAPTER 5: PHILOSOPHY OF DEVO 33
CHAPTER 6: THE EARLY YEARS 39
CHAPTER 7: DEVO, THE FILM MAKERS 45
CHAPTER 8: AT THE CRYPT 51
CHAPTER 9: JOCKO HOMO 55
CHAPTER 10: PUNK OR NEW WAVE? 59
CHAPTER 11: IN NEW YORK CITY 65
CHAPTER 12: IN LOS ANGELES 69
CHAPTER 13: DAVID BOWIE & BRIAN ENO 75
CHAPTER 14: SPUDBOYS VS. THE MUSIC INDUSTRY 79
CHAPTER 15: IN GERMANY 83
CHAPTER 16: ARE WE NOT MEN? 89
CHAPTER 17: LEAVING AKRON 95
CHAPTER 18: THE AKRON SOUND 99
CHAPTER 19: DEVO & NEIL YOUNG 113
CHAPTER 20: DUTY NOW FOR THE FUTURE 117
CHAPTER 21: FREEDOM OF CHOICE 123
CHAPTER 22: GETTING SOME SATISFACTION 129
CHAPTER 23: NEW TRADITIONALISTS 135
CHAPTER 24: SO LONG WARNER BROTHERS 139
CHAPTER 25: THROUGH BEING COOL 143
CHAPTER 26: AN ENIGMA 146

CHAPTER 27: **MUTATO MUZIKA** 151
CHAPTER 28: **A REUNION** 157
CHAPTER 29: **THE NEW DEVO** 161
CHAPTER 30: **BEAUTIFUL WORLD** 167
CHAPTER 31: **HALL OF SPUDS** 171
EPILOGUE 175
BIBLIOGRAPHY 179
NOTES 181
INDEX 193

▶ INTRODUCTION

Cleveland rocks, we're told. And so does nearby Akron. In 1986, Cleveland was selected as the site of the Rock and Roll Hall of Fame. The museum was built in the city, in large part, due to pioneering deejay Alan Freed, who worked behind the microphone at radio stations in both Akron and Cleveland.

The city of Akron has always struggled to maintain its own identity as a result of the large shadow of nearby Cleveland, which is situated just 45 miles to the north. Due to the proximity, Akron stood out – for many years – as the largest city in the United States without its own local television newscast.

Founded in 1825, Akron was named after the Acropolis, a majestic landmark in Athens, Greece. Akron was the highest point on the Ohio & Erie Canal, which by 1832 had connected Lake Erie to the Ohio River. Akron quickly grew around the 21 hand-operated locks that raised and lowered the canal's water level, which allowed the canal boats to proceed. With the process of passing through the city taking a full six-hours, the crews of these vessels had time to unwind, visit taverns and spend money. These man-made canals were also crucial in distributing Akron-made products such as agricultural reapers, clay pipes and oatmeal.

From its humble beginnings as a canal town, Akron soon emerged as an industrial center whose growth was tied to advances in transportation. With the rise of the automobile industry at the start of the 20th century, the city became a boomtown. From 1910 to 1920, Akron was the fastest-growing city in the entire nation as the city's population tripled to 208,000.

Akron was transformed into the Rubber Capital of the World, as virtually every major American tiremaker was headquartered in the city. For more than eight-decades, auto and truck tires were produced in Akron by companies such as Goodyear, Goodrich, General, Firestone, Seiberling and Mohawk. At one point, nearly two-thirds of all tires sold in the U.S. were manufactured in the city.

Much of the city's workforce had migrated from the Appalachian hills of West Virginia and western Pennsylvania. Many workers were first-generation immigrants from Eastern Europe. The smoke-belching factories even lured future actor Clark Gable, who earned $95 per week working at Firestone. Workers lived in neighborhoods that were named Goodyear Heights and Firestone Park, while their children attended Goodrich Junior High and Firestone High. And as fortunes were made, graceful mansions and grand estates were built on the city's northwest side.

In celebration of the charcoal-colored compound essential to tire-making, Akron was nicknamed the Rubber City. The local college football team played their games at the Rubber Bowl. In the 1930s, Akron was also home to an annual formal gala, the Rubber Ball, which was staged in the aptly named Rubber

Worker at an Akron tire plant in the 1940s.

Room nightclub, located in the Portage Hotel. The glitzy affair attracted the city's movers and shakers who dressed in elaborate outfits made completely out of rubber. The hotel was also the site of the founding of the United Rubber Workers union in 1935. That same year, dance marathons were outlawed in the city after one competition continued for several weeks.

The city was also the birthplace of Alcoholics Anonymous and the one-time home of Civil War-era abolitionist John Brown. And despite the claims from two other cities, Akron is also considered the birthplace of the hamburger. In 1885, when Akron restaurateur Charles Menches set up a booth at the Erie Agricultural Fair in Hamburg, New York, he introduced the soon-to-be beloved hamburger, 75-years before Ray Crock began expanding McDonald's into an international chain.

For decades, Akron was also the center of the sports world in three events. From 1962 to 1998, the Firestone Country Club hosted the World Series of Golf. Local attorney Eddie Elias founded the Professional Bowlers Association and launched the Tournament of Champions, which ran from 1965 to 1994. And after just one-year in Dayton, the Soap Box Derby made Akron its permanent home in 1935.

Northeastern Ohio was also the cradle of football. In 1920, the National Football League was established just 20-miles to the south of Akron at an auto dealership in downtown Canton, with Jim Thorpe installed as the president. In the league's inaugural season, the Akron Pros won the first championship. And while Knute Rockne played for the Akron Indians in 1914, John Heisman – the namesake of college football's Heisman Trophy – was fired by Buchtel College in Akron for his overly aggressive demeanor as the team's head coach.

*   *   *   *   *   *

In the 1950s, Akron offered a comfortable slice of postwar middle America. With the emergence of car culture and the construction of a national interstate highway system, the demand for tires remained strong. The city was home to numerous drive-in theaters, bowling alleys, roller rinks, drive-in restaurants and a popular amusement park with roller coasters and a large bandstand that featured musical acts and offered plenty of room for dancing, Summit Beach Park. A bustling downtown boasted two large department stores that proudly faced each other on the same street. The city also embraced fine arts with the world class art museum and a local orchestra.

Meanwhile, a new musical genre would soon take Northeastern Ohio by storm thanks to deejay Alan Freed. Raised in Salem, about an hour east of Akron, Freed was credited with popularizing the term "rock and roll." After a series of radio jobs, including as the host of a classical music show in nearby Youngstown, he was hired in 1945 by WAKR in Akron, whose studio was situated in the basement of the city's tallest building. At the station, Freed played contemporary pop music for the first time in his career. Initially hired as a news reporter, he was given his own show after the scheduled announcer had called off.

With Freed emerging as a local media star, his salary tripled in just two-years. Amassing a loyal following of teens and young adults, he set local ratings records in Akron. Often at odds with the station ownership, Freed played unapproved, non-playlist records by the latest jump-blues and hot jazz artists. On Saturdays, he hosted a popular program, *Request Review*, which featured an in-studio audience of dancing teens.

Terminated in 1950 after demanding one too many raises, Freed was immediately hired by a competing Akron station that was located across the street from WAKR. However, he was forced to quit after just one day behind the microphone when his former employer enforced the terms of his employment contract. Freed had signed radio's first-ever non-compete clause in 1948 and was prohibited from working at another radio station within a 75-mile radius for a period of one-year should he quit or be fired.

Freed returned to the radio airwaves in June 1951 at WJW in Cleveland as the host of an overnight classical music show.

Alan Freed at WAKR in Akron.

During this period, deejays were permitted to select the music they played. On the advice of close friend Leo Mintz, Freed started playing R&B, blues and doo-wop music. Mintz had observed a new trend of white teenagers requesting records by contemporary black artists at his busy, downtown Cleveland store, Record Rendezvous. With Freed naming his radio show, *The Moondog Rock And Roll House Party*, he quickly dominated the Cleveland-Akron airwaves.

Taking advantage of his radio pulpit, Freed also began staging concerts. He gained national notoriety when he organized an ill-fated show at a Cleveland hockey arena on March 21, 1952 – the Moondog Coronation Ball. The unprecedented event drew blacks and whites alike, and is considered the first-ever rock and roll concert. As *Life* magazine reported: "So they came. By foot. By bicycle. By streetcar and by bus. They came from beyond Cleveland, too, from Akron, from Canton, from all over the industrial north of Ohio, many of them the children of the great black northern migration, just a generation removed from the farm, from Mississippi and Arkansas and Louisiana and the holy hell of the rural South, gathered now for the biggest party in the history of Cleveland." The concert quickly descended into chaos. After selling 25,000 tickets to a venue with a capacity of just 10,000, Freed watched helplessly from the stage as a full-scale riot erupted during the middle of the first song.

In 1954, Freed was lured to a radio station in New York City. Working at WINS, he emerged as the most powerful deejay of the decade and often overshadowed the music he played. Continuing his concert promotions on a national level, Freed toured with the top acts of the day. He also embarked on a two-year residency at New York's Paramount Theater and earned millions with his all-star revues, breaking attendance records that had been set a decade earlier by Frank Sinatra. Freed expanded his rock kingdom to include films and a syndicated radio show. He also hosted a television show on

ABC – the first-ever network rock and roll program – which predated *American Bandstand*.

In 1957, a magazine chronicled Freed's success: "Virtually overnight, this super-salesman has parlayed rock 'n' roll to a $200,000-a-year income ($2.1 million in today's dollars). As a disc jockey for New York station WINS, his program reaches 12 states and Newfoundland. On tape, he's heard in Chicago, St. Louis, Kansas City and over the powerful Radio Luxembourg throughout Europe and England." On Sunday nights, the future members of the Beatles would regularly tune into Freed's program.

Meanwhile, Freed's replacement at WAKR, Scott Muni, was later a major player in the rise of the progressive rock format in New York City. Another employee at the station, receptionist Lola Albright, also enjoyed success in the entertainment field. After playing a nightclub singer on the popular television series, *Peter Gunn*, she scored a co-starring role opposite Elvis Presley in the film, *Kid Galahad*. Another announcer at WAKR, Art Fleming (then known as Art Fazzin) later hosted the first run of the classic game show, *Jeopardy!*

During the 1960s, Akron would produce only a few nationally known musical acts, most notably Ruby & The Romantics, who topped the pop charts with "Our Day Will Come." Another local group, Jordan Christopher & The Wild Ones, recorded the first version of the garage-rock classic, "Wild Thing," a year before the Troggs released the definitive rendition of the song.

* * * * * *

Chrissie Hynde, right, performing in downtown Akron.

Over the years, many notable Akronites have proudly proclaimed their love for the city. LeBron James refers to himself as "just a kid from Akron." The Black Keys have both displayed their fondness of their Akron roots by wearing t-shirts emblazoned with the city's name. In addition, the duo's frontman Dan Auerbach opens concerts with his signature greeting, "We're the Black Keys from Akron." Likewise, Chrissie Hynde's best-selling autobiography, *Reckless: My Life As A Pretender*, was considered a love letter to her hometown. As such, the book was often criticized for devoting more than 100-pages to her formative years in Akron.

On the other hand, the members of Devo have been frequently critical of Akron and its blue-collar residents due to the hostility the band endured throughout the 1970s. Devo's

Jerry Casale once said of the Rubber City: "It's in the center of the most highly industrialized part of the United States. It's hilly, grey, like culturally stripped." The animosity was the reason behind Devo's decision not to perform in Akron for nearly thirty-years. Nevertheless, for a number of years, Casale's bandmate identified himself on Instagram as "Mark Mothersbaugh, Akronite."

▶ CHAPTER 1
MARK MOTHERSBAUGH

Best known for their yellow industrial suits and red energy domes, Devo combined robotic choreography, innovative stage sets and creative costumes with experimental electronic music and quirky, nonconformist lyrics. Challenging the boundaries of popular music in the 1970s – a period when stadium rock acts like Pink Floyd, the Eagles and Fleetwood Mac were at their peak – Devo wrote their own rules. In 1977, a music critic said of the Akron band: "Perhaps they are the antithesis of the mass-commercial world, purposefully mundane on the one hand, rejectfully scornful on the other."

A *Rolling Stone* writer concisely summed up what made Devo extraordinary in the rock world: "Devo was a self-contained concept band. They created their own music, their own costumes, their own packaging and marketing formulas, and their own unique and cynical world view. Devo was actually a futuristic protest band, whose target was nothing less than humanity itself.... They wrote and played songs that merged classic rock guitar riffs with an electronic edge that was several years ahead of the new-wave electropop synthesizer sounds of the early eighties. They dressed in baggy reactor-room anti-radiation jump suits, 3-D sunglasses, elbow and kneepads and hockey helmets (all of it implying that they had a dirty and dangerous job to do, and implicitly equating play, as in music, with work and sport). They designed their own advertisements and record sleeves, making slyly ironic uses of Fifties pop culture artifacts (again, way before anyone else did)."

Devo frontman Mark Mothersbaugh was an atypical rock star – educated, serious-minded and formally trained as a visual artist. The Mothersbaugh family had settled in the Rubber City with the prospect of finding work in the region's many tire plants. The family had left the coal mines of rural Appalachia for a more prosperous life in the suburban Akron community of Cuyahoga Falls. Robert Mothersbaugh Sr., the family's patriarch, had served in the Coast Guard during World War II. After working in sales for many years, he later operated a very successful employment agency and was active in his community. His wife, Mary, taught Sunday School classes for 41-years at Journey Covenant Church in Cuyahoga Falls.

The eldest of five children, Mark Mothersbaugh had a difficult childhood, marred by a serious vision problem that went undiagnosed. He recalled: "The teacher would say: 'Read what it says on the board,' and I'd go, 'What's a board?' Then everybody would laugh and the teacher would go, 'All right, smart man. Go to the corner.' I'd stand in the corner and wonder: How do people know the right things to say when they ask you a question like that? I knew people had some information I didn't have. One day someone saw me doing homework and told my parents, 'Maybe you should get his eyes tested.'" Visiting an optometrist, Mothersbaugh recalled sitting in the examination chair: "I couldn't read the big E on the eye chart from five-feet away."

Overnight, the seven-year-old's life changed dramatically with the aid of glasses. He recalled: "I could remember five minutes after putting on my first pair, and [my father and I] came over a hill and in the distance was the elementary school I walked to every day, and I had never seen that school before. I saw the tops of trees, I saw telephone wires and clouds and birds in the sky. I saw the sun for the first time. It was amazing.... I couldn't believe I had this amazing gift from the optometrist."

Additionally, he was no longer treated like the class clown by either his teachers or fellow classmates. Wearing his eyeglasses for the first time during the last week of second grade, he discovered a love of art: "The next day when I went to school, I was drawing trees.... The teacher said, 'You draw trees better than me,' and that one sentence was the first time she wasn't spanking me or giving me an F or sending me to the corner or the principal's office. She said something positive. And that night, I dreamt I was going to be an artist. I was certain of it after that." However, with his thick glasses and poor social skills, he was bullied and still treated as an outcast. Consequently, he had few friends and dreaded going to school.

During this period, another important event occurred in Mothersbaugh's life, which would guide him in the future. For his 7th birthday he received a Mr. Potato Head – a primitive, but popular, toy invented just five-years earlier. His fascination with the toy would later become the basis for Devo's "Spud Boy" character.

Several years later, Mothersbaugh and his friends started calling each other "spuds" and other types of vegetables as either a term of endearment or insult. While the Kennedys and other highbrow Americans would be considered thin and svelte asparagus, Mothersbaugh considered himself a somewhat dirty and boorish potato. Eventually, the spud would become an essential part of the Devo lexicon.

Like all his siblings, Mothersbaugh took piano lessons from the family's organist at their church, "Mrs. Fox." The five Mothersbaugh children were taught on the family's Hammond M3 spinet organ that their father had purchased in the 1950s. Mothersbaugh recalled: "I thought music was something my mother had invented to torture me. She made me sit at home and learn church hymns on the organ while my friends were out playing."

Eventually, Mothersbaugh discovered a useful purpose for the tedious weekly music lessons. He recalled an incident at age 13 in 1964: "I was sitting at the dinner table watching a little black and white TV and I saw the Beatles on *The Ed Sullivan Show*.... I sat there and thought 'I've been tortured with music lessons for the last five years and now I know why.' I finally had seen a practical application." Future Devo bandmate, Jerry Casale, had also watched the program. Initially inspired to be a drummer, he wanted to be the next Ringo Starr.

After the Beatles made their triumphant American television debut, the nation experienced a tidal-wave shift in the direction of popular music. During the first week of April 1964, the Beatles held down *all* five of the top-five spots on *Billboard's* Hot 100.

Meanwhile, the first Cleveland-area band to perform British

Invasion-style music was the Mods, which had formed in late-1963 after a friend returned from England, bringing back a Beatles single, "She Loves You," as well as a Beatles album. This was before any Ohio radio station had ever played a record by the Fab Four. Eventually, the Mods were renamed the Choir and would later score a regional hit with "It's Cold Outside." (Three members of the Mods/Choir would later join Eric Carmen to form the Raspberries.)

During the mid-1960s, the Beatles would perform twice in Northeastern Ohio – at Public Hall and Cleveland Stadium. After their first appearance in 1964 – which was stopped by police after screaming, over-exuberant fans rushed the stage – Cleveland Mayor Ralph Locher imposed a so-called "Beatle Ban," prohibiting rock concerts at city-owned venues for the next eighteen-months. The second Beatles show, which took place in the summer of 1966, also ground to a halt after 5,000 hysterical fans stormed the small, rickety stage, which had been erected on the infield of Cleveland Stadium during the middle of baseball season.

Inspired by the Fab Four, Mothersbaugh launched his first rock band: "We were awful, of course." He was also briefly a member of a band that featured a young, painfully shy Chrissie Hynde. She later wrote in her autobiography: "A guy from Cuyahoga Falls, Mark Mothersbaugh, was putting a band together. My brother knew his brother. He was a bespectacled oddball, but then Ohio was a breeding ground for oddballs. I was asked if I wanted to be the singer. I guess I had that kind of personality, or maybe I just looked the type. The band was called Sat Sun Mat." Although a number of written accounts have claimed that the two dated, Hynde has repeatedly insisted that she never had a boyfriend while in high school.

Tired of playing the family's traditional organ, Mothersbaugh begged his parents for a portable Farfisa organ. Eventually, they relented and bought the $280 instrument for the budding teenage rocker. (The Farfisa was heard on a number of 1960s garage-rock classics such as "Wooly Bully," "96 Tears" and "Double Shot (Of My Baby's Love).") Meanwhile, Mothersbaugh's two younger brothers would also ask their parents for musical instruments. While Bob initially received a Coral electric sitar – before switching to a standard guitar – Jim was the recipient of a set of drums.

Attending Woodridge High School, Mark Mothersbaugh took pleasure in rebelling against authority. A classmate later recalled: "They were so strict at Woodridge, and Mark and I kind of retaliated. On dress-down day, he and I would wear ties. We'd just be a little different than everyone else. Then, when my older brother went to Haight-Ashbury [in San Francisco], he brought us back some flowered shirts and Sgt. Pepper jackets. That's when the school really came down on us."

Continuing to hone his talents as an artist, Mothersbaugh won first place in a high school art exhibition with a watercolor painting. His brother, Bob, took third place. With the aid and encouragement of his high school art teacher, Mark Mothersbaugh enrolled at Kent State. Creatively inclined, he received a partial art scholarship. He recalled: "I really disliked all my school years until I got to Kent. I loved the idea that the school was so big. I could be anonymous. I didn't have to get into confrontations and fights every day."

While attending college, Mothersbaugh regrew his lengthy hair, which he had been forced to cut in high school. In a Kent

State yearbook, he is pictured sporting very long hair. (In 1975, Mothersbaugh recalled one unpleasant memory of his senior year in high school: "I went back there recently, and some [teacher] used to paddle me in '68 for having 'long hair' – his hair is longer than mine was then.")

At Kent State, Mothersbaugh developed a taste for experimental music. He recalled: "I used to go to the record store at Summit Mall in Akron, and you would have to push past cutouts of Frank Sinatra and Annette Funicello to get to this one little box that was called 'other stuff' that had Captain Beefheart and Sun Ra and Silver Apples." (One of the first electronic groups in rock music, the little-known Silver Apples had a profound influence on Mothersbaugh. The group's leader, Simeon Coxe, played a self-constructed early synthesizer.)

▶ CHAPTER 2
JERRY CASALE

Mark Mothersbaugh's future bandmate Gerald "Jerry" Casale was raised in a very traditional home in the city of Kent. His stoic father had joined the Army during World War II, landed at Normandy and won the Purple Heart. Later, he worked as a tool and die mechanic in one of the many machine shops dotting the Akron-area.

The younger Casale explained: "The '60s come along and I'm a teenager and I'm in a cultural revolution.... But I have a father who likes Frank Sinatra and Johnny Mathis, and likes clean-cut guys in suits and he's kind of politically conservative and what happens? The Beatles, the Vietnam War and Jerry, his eldest son, instead of making him proud, I start growing my hair and listening to the Rolling Stones."

As children, both Jerry and his brother, Bob, received plastic guitars as presents from their parents. A self-taught musician, Jerry Casale was drawn to the music of Elvis Presley's bassist, Bill Black, and was later influenced by Rolling Stones bassist, Bill Wyman. In his teen years, Casale was attracted to innovative and experimental musical artists, especially Bob

Dylan and Captain Beefheart. Casale recalled: "I saw every act when they were new. I saw Bowie on the Ziggy Stardust tour in Cleveland, I saw early Queen, and going back I saw the Rolling Stones, Roxy Music, the Who, the Kinks, and Jimi Hendrix twice. And Bowie did it for me. I had never seen anything like it.... It was total theatrics mixed with music." Casale would later name Bowie's *Diamond Dogs* as his favorite album. (Also in the audience at the 1972 Bowie concert in Cleveland was Chrissie Hynde.)

Enrolling at Kent State with a full scholarship in 1966, Casale initially studied 20th Century comparative literature. He recalled: "My parents had no use for the university. They were blue-collar. They were conservative. They couldn't afford to send me to a college and thought I should just get a job. There was no vote of confidence there. I wasn't somebody my father was proud of."

Like Mothersbaugh, Casale was a nonconformist who went out of his way to challenge authority. During his first few years on the Kent State campus, Casale was often harassed by fellow students for wearing his hair long. He recalled: "There was this small clique of us artsy students from places like New York, Connecticut, and Massachusetts. We dressed fashionably and grew our hair long and liked Andy Warhol and the Velvet Underground."

Casale also participated in protests against the Vietnam War. He recalled: "The political movement on campus grew my entire time there. It began with off-campus meetings of 20 students, where we were yelled at and harassed for attending such a thing. That grew into a couple hundred students the next year in the Student Union at lunchtime. That grew into a massive protest and people shouting at each other."

Eventually, Casale joined the SDS because he was looking for a more organized means to protest the war. He recalled: "I was drafted in 1967. I thought I was going to go there and die, but my doctor that had been seeing me since I was an infant had been treating me for a hernia. He filled out a ginned-up report and made it a left inguinal hernia, and that got me a deferment. I just don't think I was hard-wired to be a soldier."

At Kent State, Casale began pursuing a second major – fine arts. He once stated: "Art is intended to make people think or make people feel better. Artistic expression is the enemy of mediocrity." Joe Walsh, a student at the time, recalled: "It was a very creative time to be at Kent, and I was encouraged to be creative while I was here. I'm just so grateful that I found this little place in Ohio where creative people were all together."

Meanwhile, before Casale and Mothersbaugh became acquainted at Kent State, the two men were already familiar with each other's artwork. Finally, they met at a bar on North Water Street in downtown Kent. Mothersbaugh recalled being asked by Casale: "'Are you the guy who is putting pictures of astronauts holding potatoes all over campus?' And I was like, 'Yeah.'" Mothersbaugh added: "We started talking about what we were seeing. We decided it wasn't evolution but devolution. I had this cynical attitude about religion but the same with science. [Scientists] had ideas but a lot of it seemed not worked out. They would say that the universe is finite but they don't know what the universe looks like at the edge. We thought devolution was the common ground between science and religion."

Casale recalled: "We had really similar aesthetics and ideas about art. Then we found out that we both played music, and we started applying our art concepts to music as well. He had seen my stuff, and I had seen his. I didn't know who he was, and he didn't know who I was, but we kept wanting to meet each other because we kept doing things that were pissing everybody off." Likewise, Mothersbaugh remembered: "We clicked from the very beginning. We were both kind of like prankster outsiders."

Mothersbaugh recalled how his future bandmate would purposely engage in antagonistic behavior: "For [Casale's] senior art project... he blew up pictures of kids from his high school yearbook and hung these decals of potato men on their ears, off their glasses – just stuck 'em on their faces so it looked like insects on these people's faces. He did a gallery show like that. I went and listened to the comments: 'This can't be art. This isn't art. This is ridiculous.'" Later, when Mothersbaugh was still an undergraduate and Casale was in grad school, Casale convinced Mothersbaugh he could get away with enrolling in graduate-level classes. Consequently, the two art majors occasionally took the same class.

▶ CHAPTER 3
KENT STATE

Remarkably, the creation of Devo can be directly attributed to a violent incident that shook the nation. The opposition to the Vietnam War was at the core of the counterculture movement on America's college campuses during the late-1960s. The first anti-war protest on the Kent State campus occurred on April 14, 1965, with protesters carrying signs that read "Yankee Come Home" and "U.S. Constitution Guarantees Free Assembly."

By 1970, anti-war protests around the country had intensified. On April 20, when President Richard Nixon announced that he was expanding the war and sending forces into neighboring Cambodia to attack elements that were aligned with North Vietnam, students launched massive protests at nearly 440 U.S. universities. And weeks before the May 4th tragedy, there was widespread unrest at other campuses around Ohio, most notably at Ohio University in Athens and Ohio State University in Columbus.

The trouble at Kent State started on Friday night, May 1, when reveling protesters decided to take over and occupy North Water Street in downtown Kent. Chrissie Hynde, one of the protestors, recalled: "We took these big garbage cans from the side of the road, wheeled them into the middle of the street and set them on fire. It was an awesome sight." However, things quickly soured.

As *Time* magazine reported, "One irate motorist gunned his car's engine as if to drive through the dancers. Some students climbed atop the car, jumped on it, then led a chant: 'One-two-three-four, we don't want your war!' A drunk on a balcony hurled a bottle into the street – and suddenly the mood turned ugly. Students smashed the car's windows, set fires in trash cans, began to bash storefronts.... Police stormed into bars after midnight, turning up the lights, shouting 'Get out!' Some 2,000 more students, many of whom had been watching the Knicks-Lakers basketball game on TV, were forced into the street."

With a large demonstration planned for Saturday, alarmed authorities at Kent State attempted to diffuse the situation by quickly setting up various on-campus activities such as poetry readings, films and a concert. A performance by a pair of rock bands was planned at the Tri-Towers dormitory complex.

However, tensions were not diffused as protesters burned down the one-story, wooden Army ROTC building. The situation took a turn for the worse. *Time* reported: "Without bothering to consult Kent State authorities, Mayor [LeRoy] Satrom asked for help from the National Guard. Governor James Rhodes... quickly ordered Guardsmen transferred from points of tension in a Teamster strike elsewhere in Ohio. Within an hour, about 500 Guardsmen, already weary from three nights of duty, arrived with fully loaded M-1 semiautomatic rifles, pistols and tear gas."

On Sunday, the campus and the downtown district were in a high state of alarm. Meanwhile, Governor Rhodes arrived in Kent and chose not to close the university. Instead, he banned campus demonstrations and declared a state of emergency.

Then on Monday – the fateful date of May 4th – the unthinkable happened. Writing in her autobiography, Chrissie Hynde remembered: "Anyone who lived in Kent was heading for the common. No one wanted to miss the protest, and we were all anxious to have a look at the scene of Saturday night's fire in the daylight. The atmosphere was charged. We felt good about making our view on the war known. Our voice mattered and we felt at one with our brothers and sisters across the nation... The grassy, rolling common was teeming with students. I'd never seen it so packed. I couldn't even make out what was left of the burned-down ROTC building. I pushed my way through the crowd."

Jerry Casale recalled: "It was the first warm day of spring. There were a few buds on the trees, the sky was blue. The protest started and within moments the National Guard came over the hill like some cheesy Hollywood war movie." *Time* magazine reported: "It seemed that the campus atmosphere had settled. Shortly after noon, nearly 1,000 protestors had gathered to challenge and harass the young Guardsmen. In addition to the active protestors, another 2,000 spectators kept their distance as they watched the unfolding tragedy. Then the outnumbered and partially encircled contingent of Guardsmen ran out of tear gas." Then without explanation, the guardsmen aimed their rifles at the protestors and began firing. Casale described the scene as he stood near Taylor Hall: "We had no idea there was live ammunition in those guns. We didn't know what the hell they were doing." Casale's future bandmate, Bob Lewis, was also nearby, but in a safer spot.

Chrissie Hynde, meanwhile, was standing off to the side when she heard the sound of rifles, which confused her at first. Joe Walsh was within several-hundred feet of the shootings. He recalled that upon hearing gunfire, "everybody stopped dead in their tracks, knowing what it was, but asking each other what that sound was anyway. I got to the site 30 seconds after it happened." In all, four students were killed and nine were injured. Mark Mothersbaugh was a few blocks from the shootings, working at a downtown Kent art studio.

The campus was completely shut down and remained closed for a month. While the war in Southeast Asia continued to rage, the Kent campus eventually re-opened. Another consequence of the downtown riots came in the form of a city-wide referendum on the ballot in November 1970. The residents of Kent were asked to decide whether or not to prohibit live music from the bars within the city limits. The so-called "entertainment ban" was defeated by a margin of 3,350 to 2,222 votes. It would take three-decades for enrollment at Kent State University to recover to pre-May 4th levels.

Years later, Hynde revealed: "I don't think (the shooting) was a conspiracy or intended; it was a big mistake. I don't know why the National Guard was brought in and why they were guarding 4 inches of charcoal from a burned-down [ROTC] building with loaded rifles. That's where the problem was. I never figured out who sanctioned that great idea. I don't know why they were standing there armed at all. Students were going to turn in their folders for half-term on a normal Monday morning."

The protests and subsequent shootings had a profound effect on Casale, who was forced to rethink his world view: "It was a fork in the road, and it changed me and it sent something through my body that was like battery acid.... You had two choices. Either you have a creative response in one way or another, or you give in and become one of the pod people and just shut up and go to work and toe the line." Likewise, Bob Lewis recalled: "May 4 derailed a lot of people from the track they were on, so they were looking around for alternative ways, and creativity is one of the ways you can keep your sanity."

Additionally, Casale insisted: "Everything was falling apart. Everything was de-evolving. All these ideals that had been spouted, all the bright projections about a high-tech future, had started to be clearly not the case.... Before the shootings, I was probably a pseudo-hippy. After that, it was more like Alice Cooper – no more Mr. Nice Guy. I got a haircut."

Similarly, Mothersbaugh had a sudden realization about how society worked and concluded that the act of protesting was meaningless: "Having been there for the shootings made us feel like rebellion was obsolete. You couldn't change things that way. So we thought about who does change things and we started paying attention to Madison Avenue." Casale later revealed: "That's when Devo was born. We became an insular, parallel world: I started talking about common people – the unwashed, who believed the illusions fed to them by government and schools – as spuds, pinheads and huboons: half-humans, half-apes."

Meanwhile, in the aftermath of the shootings at Kent State, Casale and Lewis began formulating a theory of "de-evolution." Casale recalled: "We were intrigued by this goofy Yugoslav writer Oscar Kiss Maerth who theorized that man descended from a line of brain-eating apes. Hey, why not?" Maerth had written the controversial book, *The Beginning Was The End*, four-years before it was published in 1971 while he was in seclusion at the Tsin San Buddhist monastery in China.

In the summer of 1972, Lewis and Casale, along with their girlfriends and friend Gary "General" Jackett, spent a summer in San Clemente, California. Both men wound up writing for a Los Angeles arts magazine, *LA Staff*. During this period, Lewis – whose plan to earn a Ph.D. in anthropology was derailed by the May 4th shootings – published an early Devo treatise in the magazine. In the piece, he postulated: "So it is that the Devo-tees believe that only in a reaffirmation of the organic impulse, and the subsequent realization of the basic physiological facts which are the functioning components of man's destiny-cluster can the horror of cybernetic man be avoided." In another article for the magazine, the pair interviewed former teen idol, Rick Nelson.

▶ CHAPTER 4
DEVO'S DEBUT

Mark Mothersbaugh and Jerry Casale had dramatically different musical backgrounds. As Casale recalled: "I started playing the blues: classic rural blues, electric Delta blues, Chicago blues.... Mark was playing in a band that did Yes and Emerson, Lake & Palmer covers. He had long hair down to his waist, and... he'd sit there behind a stack of keyboards."

In the early-1970s, Mothersbaugh had formed a band, Flossy Bobbitt, with drummer Mike Powell. In addition to playing a variety of keyboards – including a Hammond B-3 organ, a Mellotron and a Farfisa – Mothersbaugh owned the only mini-Moog synthesizer in Akron. (Years later, Mothersbaugh became good friends with the instrument's creator, Bob Moog, and Devo would appear in the company's ads.)

During this period, Casale and Mothersbaugh first began collaborating on music. Mothersbaugh had already been composing songs with another future Devo bandmate, Bob Lewis. Lewis was an anthropology major at Kent State and had previously played basketball under notorious coach Bobby Knight at Cuyahoga Falls High School, years before Knight was hired by the University of Indiana.

After returning from California, Casale joined a popular Kent-based electric blues group that regularly performed at the Kove – the oddly named 15-60-75, which was better known as the Numbers Band. During this period, Casale, along with Bob Lewis and Peter Gregg, recorded several pre-Devo songs at a rudimentary studio in their apartment building in Kent. (Gregg – a roadie for Joe Walsh – was using the stage name, Coupe de Ville). A few more recording sessions would follow.

The small apartment complex, which was located about one-mile west of the Kent State campus above a pizza shop, was an artistic oasis. At one point or another in the early-1970s, a number of local rockers lived in the same apartment building, including Joe Walsh, Mark Mothersbaugh, Chris Butler of Tin Huey and the Waitresses and Chrissie Hynde's brother, Terry, who was in the Numbers Band.

Soon after, the first version of Devo performed at the annual Kent Creative Arts Festival – which had been staged on and off since 1950. However, Casale recalled that he and Lewis didn't really have a band at the time: "It was like something out of a *Little Rascals* show. You know: we can do it, we can put on a show. I've got an amplifier, you've got a hammer!"

Casale shared his vision for the band with Mothersbaugh: "I told him I wasn't interested in being in a covers band, that I only wanted to do something original. I basically propagandized Mark with all my 'devolution' theories and he assimilated it all really quickly. Then we started writing 'devolved' music together."

As to what to call themselves, Mothersbaugh explained: "We were looking for a name for the band. We're going, 'Well, here's Art Deco, Art Nouveau... we're like Art-De-veau.' We just kept shortening it until we had Devo. And everybody went, 'That's it!'" For their first performance, the group chose the moniker, Sextet Devo. Mothersbaugh revealed: "We thought, 'If we called it Sextet Devo, we can trick 'em into thinking we're a jazz band letting us play at this jazz festival.'"

Although he was considered too mainstream for Devo, Fred Weber was hired as the group's lead vocalist. He had previously been a member of both the Measles (after the departure of Joe Walsh) and one of the most popular Kent bands of the '60s, the Chancellors. Although Jerry Casale had wanted to be the singer, Lewis doubted his bandmate's vocal abilities.

With Lewis on guitar, Casale on bass and Mothersbaugh on keyboards and guitar, the impromptu outfit was rounded out with Jerry Casale's younger brother, Bob, on rhythm guitar and keyboards and former Numbers Band member, Rod Resiman, on drums. This lineup would perform only a single time.

Devo's first-ever performance took place on April 18, 1973, at Kent State University's Recital Hall, located inside the Music & Speech building. Mothersbaugh wore an oversized ape mask and dark sunglasses throughout the entire show. The sparsely attended show featured an unusual assortment of songs, including "Mr. Jingeling," which was a tribute to a popular, elf-like Christmastime character created by the Cleveland department store chain, Halle's. Throughout the performance, the members of Devo were purposely hostile and attempted to alienate the crowd – something they would often repeat over the next several years. Two of Weber's musician friends were in attendance, with one of them later commenting, "They came out in masks and lab coats and played the most off the wall songs." A month later, Weber – who felt the group's music was too unconventional – left the band. And with growing conflicts within the band, both Rod Reisman and Bob Casale would leave as well.

Meanwhile, Casale graduated with a double major at Kent – Fine Arts and English. Due to his membership in the SDS, he was not permitted to attend the university's graduation ceremony and instead received his diploma in absentia by mail. Afterward he was hired as a part-time art instructor at the University of Akron. As a result of an unfortunate classroom incident, he taught at the institution for only one semester. During a class, Casale had been showing his students some of Mark Mothersbaugh's abstract art. However, during a break, a student thumbed through Mothersbaugh's collection of artworks, which had been left on Casale's desk, and came upon some material that she found offensive. After the student took the binder to the head of the department, Casale was dismissed from his position.

▶ CHAPTER 5
THE PHILOSOPHY OF DEVO

In a short period of time, Devo quickly gelled. With the departure of Fred Weber, Jerry Casale assumed most of the lead vocal duties. Additionally, Bob Mothersbaugh joined on guitar. Up to this point, his most notable job had been crushing rocks at a quarry in Kent. Soon after, Jim Mothersbaugh, an electronic whiz, joined on drums. Mark Mothersbaugh recalled: "[Jim] created a homemade electronic drum kit using acoustic drums with guitar pickups attached to their heads, which he'd feed into wah-wah pedals, fuzztones, and Echoplexes. It sounded really amazing, like a walking, broken-down robot."

Around this time, Bob and Jim Mothersbaugh were also members of a four-man working rock band, the Jitters. In 1973, they recorded a four-track demo at a studio in Cleveland. Mark Mothersbaugh played keyboards on two of the songs.

Meanwhile, the members of Devo continued to formulate their political and social philosophy. The ideology behind Devo – short for de-evolution – was formulated from a series of eclectic sources. In addition to *The Beginning Was The End* by

Oscar Kiss Maerth, the members of the group were also inspired by an oddball religious pamphlet, *Jocko-Homo Heavenbound*, which was published in 1920. (Although the members of Devo were influenced by the publication, it would be several years before anyone in the band would actually own a copy.)

Additionally, the members of Devo were especially influenced by a 1948 Wonder Woman comic book depicting a "deevolution" device in "Dr. Zool's laboratory," which was capable of reversing the evolutionary process. The comic book belonged to Bobbie Watson, the girlfriend of Bob Lewis. Lastly, the Devo ideology embraced elements of the satirical pseudo-religion, the Church of the SubGenius, which was embodied by the ever-smiling face of J. R. "Bob" Dobbs.

Devo would not perform in public again until the following year's Creative Arts Festival on April 23, 1974 – this time inside the newly built Governance Chambers on the Kent State campus. The student newspaper proclaimed: "Devo makes a triumphant return to the site of last year's spectacle." This time around, the group was better prepared.

Meanwhile, some friends of the group constructed a small, concrete-block recording studio behind a self-serve car wash at the edge of Akron. The sparingly equipped room – which was also used to store large barrels of liquid soap – was dubbed Man-Ray Studio. Devo would sporadically record at the facility over the next few years. Other local acts – including Chi-Pig, John Rader and the Immortal Porpoises – would also use the studio.

During a trip to a novelty store in nearby Canton, Mothersbaugh purchased several East German-made doll-like masks. Soon wearing one of the masks onstage, Mothersbaugh created his alter-ego – Booji Boy (pronounced boogie boy). The character symbolized the concept of never having to grow up. According to Mothersbaugh, Booji Boy is "the infantile spirit

The Numbers Band performing in downtown Akron.

of devolution." Later, Devo would close their shows with Booji Boy sitting in his wooden crib and singing in an innocent, high-pitched, childlike voice.

During this period, Jerry Casale was a member of both Devo and the Numbers Band. But the arrangement soon came to an end. Casale recalled: "Mark and I had started buying masks. One time I brought a full-head rubber ape mask with me to a [Numbers Band] gig and slipped it on before we did that Bo Diddley song 'You Can't Judge A Book By Its Cover.' The people that were dancing stopped cheering for the band, started pointing, and frontman Robert Kidney turned around and saw me in the mask. I got fired. That helped me get more serious about Devo."

Later in 1974, Devo finally began performing in clubs

around Akron and Kent. After Casale asked his former bandmate Robert Kidney for some assistance in securing a weekday gig, Devo made their nightclub debut at a popular downtown Kent nightspot, the Kove. (Despite numerous written accounts, Kidney insists that Devo never opened for the Numbers Band.) Around this time, Bob Lewis gradually abandoned his role in Devo as a performer and emerged as the group's manager.

Meanwhile, on April 4, 1975, Devo performed on the Kent State campus at the invitation of Jerry Casale's former professor, Richard Myers. A notable filmmaker, Myers staged weekly on-campus screenings of experimental and cult movies. Devo performed twice that evening, before a pair of showings of the outrageous John Waters film, *Pink Flamingos*. Admission was limited to Kent State students. For the shows, Devo was billed as "The De-evolution Band," and the members were listed as China Man, Jungle Jim, the Clown and Booji Boy (spelled Boogie Boy). This would mark the only time that Mothersbaugh would wear his Booji Boy mask for the entire performance. The group finished both of their sets with a rendition of the Little Richard classic, "The Girl Can't Help It," which was also featured in the film.

Not surprisingly, the bewildered members of the audience reacted poorly to the costumed musicians who were playing experimental music. Also in the audience was a dozen of the group's friends, including Gary "General" Jackett, a fellow art student who often aided Devo in their early endeavors. (In 1970, Jackett earned some local notoriety after he was selected to design a poster for a Kent State Arts Festival. The poster's bawdy design was deemed to be of "questionable taste" and was subsequently banned by the university.) Jackett also co-wrote an early version of the song, "Sloppy (I Saw My Baby Gettin')," which would appear on Devo's first album. Casale recalled: "He had written 'Sloppy,' and we wanted to honor him and do a rendition of it. We added some changes to the words and put the lyrics to a different kind of beat. We were never sure what it meant. It just made us laugh."

▶ CHAPTER 6
THE EARLY YEARS

Jerry Casale once stated: "We were not musicians. We were users of instruments." Over a very short period of time, the group's sound continued to evolve. As Mark Mothersbaugh recalled: "When we first started together we used windshield wipers and washing machines for our rhythm instruments. Or, like, jamming with the telephone busy signal! ... We realized that was getting too artsy after a while. It was impractical to do that in front of an audience, so we picked up a drummer when we got our first job."

Additionally, the members of the group realized they were having trouble replicating certain sounds, night after night, with their modified and non-traditional instruments. Mothersbaugh explained: "We got into experimenting with tape recorders and the toys on the market, like Radio Shack organ kits for eleven dollars, and Mattel Optigans.... We also experimented a lot with things that weren't even instruments, including electric appliances, gated TV noise... It was like having a chemistry set. After we did a record, our problem became one of making the same sound two nights in a row.... When we had to play the same songs twenty nights in a row, we had to find a way to stabilize our equipment."

Nevertheless, Devo continued to take shape as Mark Mothersbaugh and Jerry Casale emerged as the public faces of the group. Casale recalled: "Devo, from the beginning, was a collaboration, and Mark and I did everything, 50/50. So, without that collaboration, if you have four of eight cylinders not firing, you don't have a race." While Mothersbaugh composed most of the music, Casale came up with the lyrics. And while Mothersbaugh designed the group's album covers, Casale choreographed the group's stage moves. The other members usually stayed in the background and rarely spoke to the press. A rock critic once stated, "Bob Mothersbaugh... doesn't say much, but this seems generally true of people sharing an enclosed space with Casale."

More changes to the group's sound followed. Mothersbaugh recalled: "It wasn't until '75 when Jerry [Casale] took a drive to New York and saw the Ramones and other bands that we thought, 'Wow, listen how fast they're playing.' We thought, 'Our music will sound better faster.' Until then we'd been playing at Ohio unemployment speed. Punk really inspired us to fire it up a notch or two."

Also that year, two members of Devo traveled to California with a seven-song demo cassette to solicit the help of former Kent State student, Joe Walsh, who was well known for his generosity. Walsh had achieved a great deal of success in the James Gang and was several months away from joining the Eagles. As Mothersbaugh recalled, "We were real excited, we said, 'This guy, although he doesn't play our kind of music exactly, I know when he hears it he'll realize it's great stuff and he'll help us out!' We were certain of it – 'It's going to be the big time soon!'"

In author Evie Nagy's book, *Freedom Of Choice*, she chronicled Walsh's meeting with the two members of Devo: "Mark and Jerry drove out to L.A. to try to get a demo tape into the hands of labels. Exploiting a Kent State connection, they stayed on soon-to-be Eagle Joe Walsh's floor, hoping the fellow Ohioan would get what they were about and lend them a hand. 'Halfway through the first song on the demo tape, he ran into the other room,' says Mark. 'Him and this other guy with really long hair, they're in the dining room smoking a joint, trying to stifle laughter.'" Amazingly, even the experimental rocker Frank Zappa – who had played at Kent State in 1973 – turned the group down. Mothersbaugh recalled: "When we played him a tape, he goes, 'You say these guys rehearse in a garage? Good. That's where they belong.'"

During this period, Mothersbaugh was still spending a great deal of his time creating art. In February 1975, his work was displayed at the Packard Gallery in Akron and included lithographed postcards and various hand-stamped prints. This also marked the first time he was interviewed by *The Akron Beacon Journal*.

Meanwhile, Devo struggled to build a following around Akron. Though polishing their songwriting, musicianship and stage act, Devo was usually met with confusion – if not outright hostility – by local audiences. Michael Heaton, a popular Cleveland newspaper columnist, was in attendance during one of the group's early shows at a Kent nightclub: "I was at the bar draining a Rolling Rock when five guys dressed in short-sleeved gas station attendant jumpsuits and safety goggles came out and started playing this loud, emphatic robot-rock. I was frozen in midsip wondering, what the... Was it a joke? An art movement or a bowel movement? They weren't laughing. Nobody in the club knew what to make of them."

Devo was met with the same reaction by Kent State students at the Rathskeller, a venue inside the student center. A professor at the university recalled: "The school lore is that they were regularly booed off the stage at the [Rathskeller]. It was at the last days of disco, and disco certainly deserved to die. But how could you put Devo's strange act in the context of John Travolta and the Bee Gees?"

Subsequently, Devo established a routine at their early shows. They would announce, "here's one by Foghat," but would instead play an original song. They would sometimes be paid to quit playing. Usually, they wouldn't be paid at all. Jerry Casale recalled: "We were called crazy, cynical, negative, clowns, Nazis. We used to laugh about being Nazi clowns.... We just pissed people off. It frightened them. Some felt sorry for us. Some people wanted to hurt us. I think most people just thought our ideas were preposterous."

Mothersbaugh described what occurred after the group was hired as a last-minute replacement by an Akron nightclub owner: "He's never heard us, only that we had a band. So he hired us, we went on stage, and he proceeded to pay us to quit. One guy who had been yelling for Aerosmith all night finally came up to me and demanded that we 'play some... Foghat.' He then ripped the Booji Boy mask off my face and ripped it to shreds. We knew we had something when we got that kind of response."

One of the group's most notorious early performances took place on Halloween night in 1975. The private party was sponsored by Cleveland radio powerhouse WMMS and was staged for several-hundred partygoers at the old WHK Auditorium. As a gag, Devo had been hired as the opening act for Sun Ra, an avant-garde jazz collective. Quickly, Devo alienated the crowd by playing an extended version of "Jocko Homo," and refused to end the song. Finally, a number of angry audience members dressed in Halloween costumes stormed the stage. In a short period of time, Devo had managed to nearly empty the large auditorium before the headlining act had played a single note.

As Casale later recalled: "They hated us from the moment we walked out. We were dressed in gray industrial jumpsuits, clear plastic masks and industrial helmets, and they wanted to hear, like, Bad Company.... and they were all drunk. Also there were two tanks of nitrous oxide.... They did not like us. It was like putting a bad acid trip on 'em. We started into 'Jocko Homo' and got attacked, literally, on stage. One guy knocked me down, grabbed the microphone, and said, 'You gonna let them stand up here and let them do this to us?' Half the crowd liked us, half wanted to kill us, and they ended fighting among themselves. Two big guys snuck around backstage and tried to come on from behind the curtain and beat us up. They had fights with our road crew, and the concert ended right there." Afterward, the members of Devo discreetly returned to the venue in their street clothes to watch Sun Ra's performance. (The concert was recorded for posterity and was belatedly released in 1992.)

▶ CHAPTER 7
DEVO, THE FILM MAKERS

On the brink of disbanding, Devo decided to expand into another creative medium – film. After reading an electronics magazine, Mark Mothersbaugh was convinced a home movie player would be commonplace in a year or two. He recalled: "In 1974, Jerry Casale, his brother Bob, and I were writing songs for Devo when our friend Chuck Statler came over with a copy of *Popular Science* magazine. On the cover, it had a picture of a young couple holding what looked like a vinyl record, except it was silver and reflective. And it said, 'Laser discs. Everyone will have them by Christmas.' Chuck had taken filmmaking classes, and then directed commercials. We wanted to make films that used our songs, so they could eventually be on laser discs. We were art students from Kent State who were influenced by Robert Rauschenberg and Andy Warhol." During his childhood, Mothersbaugh had been exposed to amateur filmmaking as his father enjoyed shooting 8mm films of the family.

Wanting to raise funds for a film project, Mothersbaugh and Casale opened a retail business at a small downtown Akron

The skyline of downtown Akron.

mall, Quaker Square. Launched in late-1974, the Unit Services Shop offered graphic design services and sold ink stamps. After saving $2,000 and receiving additional funding from a local arts patron, Mothersbaugh and Casale shuttered the business and started working on their film.

Adopting a new look for the project, the members of Devo wore matching, yellow industrial suits that were purchased from a local manufacturer, the Murdoch Company. Casale had discovered the $4 outfits while working as a graphic artist for the firm. Mothersbaugh recalled: "We ran into these suits they wore at the Goodyear plant when they were spraying dangerous chemicals. We were looking for something to wear onstage and wrapping ourselves up in these yellow things so we looked kind of looked like fast-food. Big Mac sandwiches appealed to us." As a finishing touch, the suits were accessorized with black belts and the word "DEVO" spelled out with black electrical tape.

Mothersbaugh later observed: "What we saw as being the uniform of the day was blue jeans. We thought it was ironic and moronic, at the same time, people expressing their individuality by dressing alike. We thought we would dress alike – but differently. We'd have our own mindset.... The yellow suits just looked so good because they totally exploded the myth of rock star as sex symbol." However, there were some unforeseen problems with their new stage uniforms. Jerry Casale explained: "They don't breathe at all. It is like a piece of Swiss cheese melting on a burger. When we were doing like 50-city tours in those, we would be so trim at the end of the tour. It was like kind of a weight loss program."

Devo began filming in May 1976. The project was directed by Chuck Statler, who was living in Minneapolis at the time. While majoring in film at Kent State in the early-1970s, he first met Mothersbaugh and Casale in an experimental art class. Statler had also filmed Devo's first performance at the Creative Arts Festival.

The project was shot at a number of area locales – including the Goodyear World of Rubber museum, the Governance Chambers at Kent State and a board room at a McDonald's restaurant in Akron. Statler recalled: "They had the concept for it basically all worked out. I was there mainly to point the camera and make sure that everything went properly. I was more a technical director than anything else, although since they didn't know much about the actual process of filmmaking, I had more input in those early days than on the later ones." A number of Devo associates appeared in the film, including various girlfriends and General Jackett, who pretended to play two conjoined guitars that were plugged into a vintage space heater.

The film featured two songs – a deconstructed version of the 1960s rock classic, "Secret Agent Man," which was performed onstage at J.B.'s in Kent, and the band's quirky autobiographical anthem, "Jocko Homo." General Boy, a recurrent Devo character, made his debut in the film. Dressed in a military uniform, he was portrayed by Mark's father, Robert Mothersbaugh Sr. He was selected for the role of the commander of the De-Evolutionary Army at the last minute after the scheduled actor failed to appear. Additionally, 100 Kent State students answered an ad in the student newspaper for the opportunity to appear as extras.

Meanwhile, Jim Mothersbaugh would leave Devo to start his own business. And in late-1976, Bob Casale had rejoined the group on guitar. To differentiate between Bob Mothersbaugh and Bob Casale, they assumed the stage names, Bob 1 and Bob 2. Jerry Casale would later describe his brother's integral role in the band's success: "He wasn't trying to be a frontman and he didn't play the leads. He was supplying all the glue, moving between keys and guitar and synthesizer, and playing all the things that needed to happen and doing it well, and making all the moves in our choreographed act that needed to be made and doing it well. He was a team player."

Additionally, drummer Alan Myers – soon nicknamed the human metronome – was invited by Bob Mothersbaugh to join the group. The two men were previously members of the same, local cover band.

A native of Akron, Myers attended Firestone High School. In junior high, he was good friends with classmate Jane Ashley,

Apartment building managed by Mark Mothersbaugh.

who as Jane Aire would later record for Stiff Records in England. Raised on jazz, classical music and the avant-garde rock of Frank Zappa, Myers was also influenced by the politically charged Beat writers of the 1950s such as Allen Ginsberg and Jack Kerouac. With the addition of Myers – a multi-instrumentalist – Devo now had a more focused drummer who was less reliant on experimental technology. Finally, Devo had established its classic lineup, which would remain unchanged over the next decade.

Meanwhile, the group would soon decamp at their new headquarters in Akron – an old apartment building owned by Mothersbaugh's father on South Walnut Street, just beyond the edge of downtown Akron. In exchange for a free apartment, Mothersbaugh worked as the manager and maintenance man. Soon after, a number of Mothersbaugh's friends and family members would move into the building. Often frightening the tenants, Mothersbaugh would answer his door while wearing his Booji Boy mask and speaking in a childlike voice. (Meanwhile, just 100-feet from the building, LeBron James would later attend high school and begin polishing his basketball skills.)

▶ CHAPTER 8
AT THE CRYPT

A number of Akron and Cleveland punk and new wave acts honed their sound at a tiny Akron nightclub called the Crypt. One local musician recalled: "The Crypt was a weird place. Everything was painted in flat black, it was dark and dingy. There were holes in the wall from where someone had punched it." The basement-level establishment was beset by a moldy smell and standing water on the bathroom floor. Located near the Goodyear factory complex on the city's industrial east side, the beer-and-shot dive was co-owned by a Goodyear laborer, Bill Carpenter, who poured cheap drinks for his blue-collar co-workers. Struggling to keep the business afloat after a lengthy labor strike in 1976, Carpenter was losing money.

Consequently, when members of a local hard-rock group, King Cobra, approached Carpenter about performing there, he offered them a remarkable deal – if they took over the lease payments and kept the bar open from morning to night, they could book any band they wanted. Taking on new duties as business owners and bartenders, King Cobra members Ward

Welch and Elmer Brandt spent their time pouring shots for factory workers during the day and operating a nightclub at night. Suddenly, the venue became an incubator for Northeastern Ohio acts such as Devo, Pere Ubu, the Dead Boys and the Bizzaros. In an act of mutual aid, Pere Ubu would help Devo to land gigs in Cleveland, while Devo did the same for Pere Ubu in Akron.

Ultimately, the members of King Cobra had an epiphany after attending a performance by the New York-based punk pioneers Johnny Thunders and the Heartbreakers (not to be confused with Tom Petty's band) at the Piccadilly Inn in Cleveland. Soon after, the members of King Cobra abandoned hard rock and stepped to the forefront of the new wave/punk movement as the renamed Rubber City Rebels. After losing two members, the group added Ron "Pete Sake" Mullens and Mike Hammer. Wanting a more appropriate Akron-centric stage name, Ward Welch became Rod Bent, before settling on Rod Firestone. Similarly, bandmate Elmer Brandt became Buzz Clic.

Meanwhile, the members of Devo became more jaded as they continued to encounter hostile audiences. As Mark Mothersbaugh recalled: "There were two places we could perform without fear of a fistfight or just being paid to quit. That was Pirate's Cove in Cleveland, where 35 hardcore people would show up, and the Crypt in Akron, where we always had 20 friends and four guys wanting to beat us up. When you're that ostracized and disenfranchised in your peer group and in your local culture, you turn unfriendly back. I know we didn't appear to be friendly, but it was self-defense. It was part of our manifesto to separate ourselves out; we were more like aliens

Cheetah Chrome of the Dead Boys.

making satirical comments on the culture. We took pleasure in being lightning rods for hostility and freaking people out." The Pirate's Cove was located in the Flats – a grimy industrial district along the mouth of the Cuyahoga River and the site of John D. Rockefeller's first-ever warehouse. The club had set aside Thursday nights for experimental rock acts.

At the Crypt, Devo often shared the bill with the Dead Boys, which was formed by musicians from both Akron and Cleveland. Fronted by vocalist Stiv Bators, the Dead Boys were punk-rock pioneers whose sound, ethos and attitude came to define the genre. However, the two groups were not fond of each other. As a strictly punk act, the Dead Boys were not fans of the experimental art-rock of the Spud Boys. A member of the

Dead Boys entourage stated at the time: "They have about 30 people who come all the time. And their crowd and our crowd don't mix. They yell 'Devo' while we're playing and we heckle back; everybody's yelling."

At one performance, things got very heated between the two bands after Cheetah Chrome, a member of the Dead Boys, famously pulled down Mark Mothersbaugh's jockey shorts while he sang, "Jocko Homo." Chrome was further amused when Mothersbaugh continued his choreographed routine instead of pulling up his shorts. Eventually, Mothersbaugh began taunting Chrome and a violent melee broke out between the two groups and their respective camps in the audience. Over the years, both sides of the conflict have offered differing details of what actually occurred.

Meanwhile, Devo continued to stand out from the other acts at the Crypt for another reason. Local singer-songwriter Jon Mosey recalled: "Most punk bands were not good musicians and just threw things together. But Devo were good musicians. They knew what they were doing."

After just several months in business as a music venue, the Crypt was forced to shutter its doors when the bar's owner sold the liquor license to a national chain restaurant for $14,000.

▶ CHAPTER 9
JOCKO HOMO

In December 1976, Devo recorded two tracks – "Mongoloid" and "Jocko Homo" – at Man-Ray Studio in Akron. Although the room had overhead heating, the concrete floor was ice cold, forcing Mark Mothersbaugh to play his keyboard while wearing gloves.

In early-1977, Devo pressed 1,000 copies of the single at Queen City Records in Cincinnati. The pressing was funded by two of the group's friends. Mothersbaugh described the experience: "I remember looking at them out in the sun and thinking, 'This feels like we made art....' It had the feeling of, 'Nobody knows who you are; you could disappear and no one would know it.' Then we had this record – 'Jocko Homo' and 'Mongoloid.' It was such a big deal." The members of Devo designed the seven-inch record's elaborate picture sleeve packaging, which they assembled at Bobbie Watson's apartment in the Highland Square district of Akron.

Although "Mongoloid" was the A-side of the single, the B-side, "Jocko Homo," became the group's signature song. As Mothersbaugh explained: "It was always our performance

David Thomas of Pere Ubu speaking at the Rock and Roll Hall of Fame.

stamp. It had the opportunity to be the craziest thing we did all night." Ed Barger, the group's touring soundman, recalled: "Mark wrote 'Jocko Homo' pretty much himself. It just came out of nowhere. At that point, Jerry was sort of the lead singer in the band, and Mark comes in with 'Jocko Homo' and boom, Mark was the lead singer." The song's question-and-answer lyrics were borrowed from the 1933 H.G. Wells feature, *The Island Of Dr. Moreau*. In the film, a group of mutants respond to all of Dr. Moreau's questions with the chant "Are we not men?"

Nonetheless, Devo still struggled to find traction. As Mothersbaugh recalled: "I was driving around Ohio going to record stores going, 'Hey, do you guys need another Devo record here?' and the guy would go down to the last bin where it said 'Miscellaneous' and finger through and go, 'Nope, still got the one you brought in last week!' And I'd drive thirty miles back to Akron – 'OK, well, didn't sell any today. But there's always tomorrow!'"

Mothersbaugh enjoyed driving to one of the stores, the Drome in Cleveland, where he would chat with one of the store's clerks – David Thomas of Pere Ubu who was calling himself Crocus Behemoth at the time. The Drome frequently staged in-store shows by punk and avant-garde groups such as Pere Ubu, the Pagans, Destroy All Monsters and Devo.

Meanwhile, Devo's long-awaited 10-minute film, *In The Beginning Was The End: The Truth About De-Evolution*, made its premiere at the Akron Art Institute on March 12, 1977. The presentation, which also featured a poet and a painter, was billed as "an afternoon of music, discussion and improvisation devoted to ideas in contemporary art." There was no review of the film in any of the local papers.

One week later, the film was screened at the Ann Arbor Film Festival. It won the prize for best short film. As a result of the publicity, Devo began garnering some national attention. Soon after, the group would open their shows by first airing the film.

Back in Akron, Devo continued to experiment at Man-Ray Studio. During one jam session, the group attempted to play a rendition of the Rolling Stones song, "Paint It Black," but quickly shifted into "Satisfaction." The song's riff came from something that Bob Casale heard while working at his day job in the radiology department at Robinson Memorial Hospital in the nearby city of Barberton. At first, Devo performed the song at their shows at a much slower tempo. Later in 1977, Devo released a second single, "(I Can't Get Me No) Satisfaction"/ "Sloppy (I Saw My Baby Getting)."

▶ CHAPTER 10
PUNK OR NEW WAVE?

Festering in the musical fringes of the urban enclaves of New York City and Los Angeles as well as the Rust Belt cities of Detroit and Cleveland, punk rock represented a working-class backlash against the manufactured stars of arena-rock and disco. At around the same time, punk was also emerging in London. As a stab against the rock establishment, the members of the Sex Pistols wore t-shirts that read "I Hate Pink Floyd."

Punk rock was a do-it-yourself movement that was embraced by music aficionados and disaffected outsiders. The music had its origins in the garage-rock of the mid-1960s as well as early avant-garde acts like the Velvet Underground and Captain Beefheart.

In the late-1980s, a *Washington Post* music writer examined the origins of the genre: "Punk rock was fashioned in Manhattan in the mid-'70s, but it was often assembled from parts made in Ohio. Such seminal New York outfits as the Contortions, the Feelies, and Teenage Jesus And The Jerks relied on recent immigrants from Ohio. In fact, many of those musicians had done time in a little-known Cleveland band, Rocket From The Tombs, or its successor, Pere Ubu." And in 1973, before the genre had a name, a little-remembered Cleveland rock group called the Punks were playing proto-punk music and were compared to the New York Dolls and Iggy Pop and the Stooges.

There was one question that frequently followed Devo in the 1970s – were they a punk or new wave act? Although Devo was eventually lumped into the new wave camp, Jerry Casale insisted: "We were punk in the true sense of the word 'punk.' We challenged illegitimate authority and challenged politically correct thought, but from a base of knowing things and reading and looking at things and having new ideas. Our whole response was a response to the state of American culture." Similarly, Bob Casale proclaimed: "The only way we fit into punk at all, was we had a pissed-off attitude/disregard for authority. But it was intellectual. It wasn't anarchistic or negative, it was making fun of everything that was stupid."

However, Devo was often spurned by both punk acts like the Dead Boys and art-rock outfits like Pere Ubu. Jerry Casale recalled: "Pere Ubu didn't like us.... They didn't have a sense of humor, and they were really disturbed by Devo's kind of smartass sense of humor. And that we were also self-effacing; we'd make fun of ourselves, so nobody could make fun of us, because we had already built that in by being clowns and wearing stupid things like yellow suits. So they really found us disturbing."

The origin of the term "punk rock" isn't clear. Rock journalists Lester Bangs and Dave Marsh of *Creem* magazine have both claimed they coined the term. It was Marsh who was the first to use the term in print at *Creem*, when he reviewed a comeback show by the 1960s group, Question Mark & The Mysterians, best known for their chart-topping hit, "96 Tears." However, *Punk* magazine co-founder John Holmstrom has argued: "In 1975, *Creem* magazine would call anything remotely hard 'punk,' and that included Alice Cooper, the MC5 and the Dictators.... [And] I remember getting copies of *NME* in the summer of '75 and they were calling AC/DC, the Bay City Rollers and Eddie and the Hot Rods punk rock. I remember seeing a big article on Eddie and the Hot Rods saying, 'Here comes punk,' but they weren't punk rock then, they were doing 'Wooly Bully.'"

Holmstrom recalled: "The word 'punk' goes back to the '60s, but we were calling it punk rock." First published in New York City at the start of 1976, *Punk* magazine was the first publication to chronicle the new musical phenomena. Another of the magazine's co-founders, Legs McNeil, was credited with suggesting the name: "I said why don't we call it *Punk*. In the early '70s there were all these TV shows like *Kojak* and *Columbo*. When they caught the bad guy at the end, they'd say, 'Hey, punk.'"

Meanwhile, there was a simmering rivalry between American and British punk acts during the early years of the movement. Steve Jones of the Sex Pistols said in 2022: "I like the Ramones; don't get me wrong. But it was different than the English punk. That New York thing and the English thing is always debated; everybody claims they invented punk."

Being labeled a punk act had a major career downside. At the time, few radio stations or concert venues wanted anything to do with punk rock. Debbie Harry of Blondie once claimed:

"Bands didn't want to be called punk because they wanted to get on the radio. I remember journalists in Chicago being afraid to talk to me because they thought I was a punk. They were afraid that I was going to beat them."

Consequently, in 1977, Seymour Stein, the owner of Sire Records, began using the term, *new wave,* to describe one of the acts on his label, Talking Heads. Stein wrote in his autobiography, "We needed all the help we could get, so I stumbled on the idea of new wave. Pilfered from the French cinematic movement Novelle Vague. I didn't know if I first read it somewhere or heard it in a conversation, but it popped into the air and became my standard telephone spiel to win over every plugger, program director, and hippie jock, 'No, Talking Heads aren't *punk*,' I kept telling everyone, 'They're new wave!' Ain't the art of selling all about perception? .... Plus, it was broadly true; Talking Heads didn't sound *anything* like the Ramones or the Dead Boys.... The new wave term caught on fast because so many other publications, managers, and record labels buzzing around the same scene had to tease the same long-haired gatekeepers of top-40 radio... And it was effective. There hadn't [been] so much hair chopping since the recruitment centers of the Vietnam War. The idea of 'new wave' was so successful in changing perceptions." Nevertheless, some bands did not appreciate being lumped into the new wave camp. Such was the case at the three-day US Festival in 1983, when U2 demanded to play on Rock Day instead of New Wave Day.

Quickly, the terms *punk* and *new wave* became part of the musical lexicon. In 1980, "It's Still Rock And Roll To Me" by Billy Joel was the first top-40 hit that referenced both punk and new wave. And on the 1981 George Harrison album, *Somewhere In England*, new wave is mentioned in the track, "Blood From A Clone." That same year, Blondie referred to punk rock in the chart-topping hit, "Rapture."

▶ CHAPTER 11
IN NEW YORK CITY

In the spring of 1977, Jerry Casale headed to New York City to book some Devo shows at the notorious punk/new wave venue, CBGB's. Casale realized that the city "was the perfect atmosphere for de-evolution. New York was what we were talking about, it was really devolving, and it was frightening and intense there. At that point, the city was a shithole, but perfect for the punk scene. The anger and frustration was palpable."

Arriving in New York a few weeks later, the members of Devo found the experience eye-opening. Mark Mothersbaugh recalled: "By that point, because we had been so insulated in Ohio, we were kind of like our own Midwestern Aborigine tribe that talked about spuds as comrades and 'high Devo' and 'low Devo.' And we were dressed in yellow plastic hazardous waste outfits instead of tattered blue jeans and T-shirts."

During the visit, the band had a celebrity encounter. Mothersbaugh recalled: "I remember early on in New York, we met William Burroughs. I went to his place in a funky part of town. He walked with a cane, because he was a little frail. There were people lying in front of his building, they'd harass you to give 'em money. When we got in his apartment, he took his cane and turned the handle, pulled out a fifteen-inch dagger and said, 'I'm waiting to use this on that guy down there that keeps hassling me.' It was pretty gritty."

The first Devo show at CBGB's took place on May 23. During one of the performances, the members of Devo got into another scuffle with the members of the Dead Boys. As Casale recalled: "[We] got into a fight with the Dead Boys. The crowd loved it. It had nothing to do with music – it was the aliens against the spuds. The Dead Boys attacked us during 'Jocko Homo'.... We continued to play all through the fight and ended up looking good. Mark offered himself up first, being in the front line." Afterward, the bad blood between the two Northeastern Ohio bands had finally been alleviated. Apparently, the Dead Boys hadn't expected Devo to fight back.

The following day, Devo played at another New York venue, Max's Kansas City. Blondie drummer Clem Burke recalled the reaction to Akron's Spud Boys: "They were playing to audiences brought up on the New York Dolls and they were a total antithesis of that. They weren't your classic leather pants and twinkie shoes rock band – they were already wearing those yellow jumpsuits. They raised a lot of eyebrows."

After one of the shows in New York, Mothersbaugh had an unlikely encounter with John Lennon. Mothersbaugh was resting in the band's van when the incident occurred: "[Lennon] was with Ian Hunter from Mott The Hoople. They were so drunk, they were holding each other up. Lennon stuck his head though the van window, his face right up close, and started [singing] part of 'Uncontrollable Urge' at me. I'd written that song as a homage to 'She Loves You' and 'I Want To Hold Your Hand.' I'd seen the Beatles on *The Ed Sullivan Show* when I was twelve and it had changed everything for me." Later, the members of Devo wound up at Debbie Harry's apartment where her Blondie bandmate, guitarist Chris Stein, took photos of both bands for a New York music magazine.

While in New York, Devo was offered a recording contract. Bob Mothersbaugh recalled: "Somebody from a record company approached us and said, 'I'd like to put you guys out on my label. Do you have girlfriends with jobs who can support you?' We said, 'Well, we think we'll wait for a better offer!'" Returning to Ohio, Devo began performing around the state.

Devo was not the only Akron band that was forced to travel to New York in order to find appreciative audiences. Nick Nicholis of the Bizarros recalled: "There was really not enough of a scene here, ever. It just got glamorized in the press. Chi-Pig, the Action, Hammer Damage and just about everybody played New York regularly and made all kinds of money. The next night they'd be back home playing for $20 to $30."

In Northeastern Ohio, Devo continued to receive negative press. A *Cleveland Plain Dealer* music critic wrote: "Devo are another batch of Akron weirdos, once described to me by a well-known local radio personality as 'the only band I've wanted to pull the plug on. Too conceptual to really be tabbed punk, the band centers around the theme that man has not evolved from the ape, but is devolving *into* one." And Jerry Casale complained to a reporter for *The Akron Beacon Journal,* "We got pretty lousy feedback to our music from the Akron area. As far as Akron is concerned, we're a bunch of people who can't play real music. The bottom line to your story is gonna be, 'Local band makes it big without local support.'"

In early-July, Devo headed back to the East Coast – for a show in Philadelphia and, then, New York City. They played three shows at Max's Kansas City and shared a bill with the Cramps, a self-described psychobilly band led by Lux Interior, who was born and raised in the Akron area.

After one of the shows, Devo was invited by record executive Kip Cohen of A&M Records to perform a showcase show in Los Angeles. The band was offered $2,000 to make the trip. Cohen was best known at that point for signing the Tubes. However, Devo wanted to hone their stage show and spent the next several weeks whipping their sound into shape before heading to the West Coast.

▶ CHAPTER 12
IN LOS ANGELES

The members of Devo felt they were prepared for their major label audition. Packed into a 1970 Ford Econoline van, Devo arrived in Los Angeles during the last week of July. For their showcase, the group performed two shows on July 25 at the legendary Starwood nightclub on the Sunset Strip. Before taking the stage, the band screened their film, *The Truth About De-evolution*.

Kip Cohen was clearly not impressed and decided to pass on the band. Casale recalled: "We came out here and quickly dispelled the notion that we were the new Tubes. When A&M saw how extreme, minimal, and hardcore it was, they didn't know what to make of it. We were the *new* in new wave."

A year later, Cohen would explain: "This was at a time when America was trying to decide whether it was going to stomach new wave or throw it back across the ocean.... They became an instant success on the L.A. club scene. But when I closed my eyes and got away from the visual antics, I was having a hard time hearing a third chord."

Although Cohen was not enamored by Devo's quirky songs

or choreographed stage show, Los Angeles music fans were clearly intrigued by the Midwestern visitors and wondered how it was possible that the band – with its well-rehearsed multimedia show – seemed to have appeared out of nowhere. Other record labels were also intrigued. Casale recalled: "Every record company started coming around, every agent, every manager. And of course, they were all pitching horribly onerous deals but, you know, it was happening, there was action, and I loved action."

Backstage at one of the Starwood shows, the members of Devo met proto-punk singer Iggy Pop, who was already a fan of the band. Surprisingly, he was already performing one of the group's songs, "Praying Hands," at his shows. Pop explained that he and Bowie were regularly listening to a Devo demo cassette given to them after a performance at the Agora in Cleveland, when Bowie had filled in as a keyboardist in Pop's band. Although stories widely vary as to how the cassette wound up in the hands of Pop and Bowie, the Devo tape was likely given to them by Susan Aylward – the wife of Michael Aylward, who was the guitarist of the Akron new wave band Tin Huey – at Swingos, a legendary Cleveland hotel where touring rockers would usually stay. (In another version of the story, a member of Devo gave the tape to drummer Clem Burke of Blondie, the opening act for Iggy Pop.) What isn't disputed is the fact that Pop initially listened to the Devo tape before later playing it for Bowie.

Also at the Starwood show was Pop's friend, singer/dancer Toni Basil (who in 1982 would score a number-one hit with the single, "Mickey"). Soon after, Basil and Jerry Casale began dating. With her experience in the entertainment business, she helped the band secure additional gigs and offered to introduce the group to her contacts in the music industry.

Despite the disappointing experience with A&M Records, Devo decided to remain in Los Angeles in order to be close to the entertainment industry. Over the next four-months, Devo performed numerous shows on the West Coast – all while trying to land a favorable recording contract. However, Devo had another reason for staying in California. Mothersbaugh later admitted: "What we really wanted to do was start a film company. Although we knew our foot in the door was going to be as a musical band, we actually came out here hoping that we were going to get to do features."

Meanwhile, Iggy Pop invited Devo to stay and rehearse at his home in Malibu. While the members of Devo practiced their songs in the living room of Pop's oceanside home, he would often take the microphone and sing over the music with improvised lyrics. (Recordings of these informal collaborations were never released.)

However, Pop had an ulterior motive – he wanted to record the group's songs. Mothersbaugh recalled: "He wanted to record our first album before we did. I was like, 'No, we want to do it first,' and he was like, 'Shut up, this would be good for you.' He was crazy during that time." Meanwhile, during this period, Pop was completing the final mixes for his solo album, *Lust For Life*.

A week or so later, Devo headed north to San Francisco. Playing at Mabuhay Gardens, the group attracted large, enthusiastic audiences. At the club, Devo met a number of celebrities, including classic rocker Neil Young, who asked Devo to appear in a movie he was planning to make, *Human Highway*.

* * * * * *

Returning to Los Angeles in mid-October 1977, Devo played at some of the city's most influential clubs, including the Hollywood Palladium and the Whisky a Go-Go. At one show, Devo shared a bill with Blondie and a popular local punk band, the Germs. At a post-concert party, future Go-Go's vocalist Belinda Carlisle tried to engage the members of Devo in conversation but had a change of heart. Writing in her autobiography, she recalled: "I was a huge fan of Devo, but I was intimidated around Mark Mothersbaugh and the other guys. It wasn't for any other reason than that they were smart college graduates who had a well-thought-out vision, and I feared not understanding whatever it was they were talking about."

As for Devo's reaction to the landscape of Los Angeles, Casale explained: "We'd seen the picture postcards of L.A. and we believed it, and we came out and it was just one long stretch of sprawl and yellow sludge, you know? And it was horrifying. And we couldn't believe that all of Hollywood, that was highly touted as the Mecca to all musicians, looked like Cuyahoga Falls, Ohio, except worse. Yeah, it was just a bigger cesspool of a place."

On Halloween, Devo played for a large, receptive audience at the Starwood – exactly two-years after their disastrous performance in Cleveland. Outside, a riot erupted after the promoter had oversold the concert and angry fans were refused entrance.

At the same time Devo was playing their brand of innovative music in Los Angeles, San Francisco and New York, the largest nightclub in the Akron area – the Big Apple – was drawing 2,000 people every Friday and Saturday night for the opportunity to pack the dance floor as the deejay played disco records. This was the era of *Saturday Night Fever*, and there was little room on the pop charts for electronic, new wave artists like Devo. (Later, the infamous lighted dance floor from *Saturday Night Fever* would be acquired by a buyer from Akron.)

▶ CHAPTER 13
DAVID BOWIE & BRIAN ENO

Returning to New York City, shortly before Thanksgiving in 1977, to play some shows at Max's Kansas City, Devo was approached by David Bowie. Taking the stage and calling the group "the band of the future," Bowie announced to the crowd that he would be working with Devo: "I'm going to produce them in Tokyo this winter!" The comment came as a huge surprise to the group. Casale, who had witnessed Bowie transform himself into Ziggy Stardust less than three-years earlier, finally felt a level of achievement.

Mark Mothersbaugh remembered: "Then afterwards, he said, 'Yeah, I really want to produce you guys. The only thing is, I'm up for this movie called *Just A Gigolo*. If I get it, I have to go to Berlin for a couple months. So that would push it off.' And we go, 'Well, we don't even have anywhere to go when we leave here.' We're homeless, you know – we don't know what we're gonna be doing for those two months. The next week, we played again, and Robert Fripp and Brian Eno came. And they invited us over to Robert Fripp's house. And he fed us. And they both said, 'We would want to produce you guys if you were up for it.' And we said, 'Well, Brian, David Bowie last week said he was producing us in Tokyo!' And Brian Eno starts going, 'He's full of shit.' At the time I didn't know that Brian Eno was kinda pissed at Bowie because he felt he didn't get credited properly on [the albums] *Heroes* and *Low*. Brian Eno said, 'Let's just go right now. Don't even worry about a record company. I'll loan you the money. We'll go over to Germany, at this studio I work at all the time – Conny Plank Studio.'" (Plank was an experimental musician who was a member of the electronic duo, Moebius & Plank. In addition to Bowie and Eno, the studio would be used by a number of notable acts such as Kraftwerk, Ultravox and the Eurythmics.)

Soon after, Eno praised Devo in an interview with *Melody Maker* magazine: "What I saw in them always happens when you encounter something new in art – you get a feeling of being slightly dislocated, and with that are emotional overtones that are slightly menacing as well as alluring. With me, that's almost a code word. I am very interested in knowing why that happens, and why that is happening now, and I spend as much time in that sort of reflection as I do in the work." And in December 1977, the group gave its first interview with *The Cleveland Plain Dealer*. The article began: "Seven months ago one [member] of the Devo quintet was on welfare. Another one was living on peanut butter and tea.... Today Fleetwood Mac comes to [the group's] concerts." Around this time, Devo started; working on two new tracks at the Different Fur Studio in San Francisco.

Returning to San Francisco a month later in mid-January 1978, Devo played a pair of shows at Mabuhay Gardens. While in the city, the members of the group attended the final concert by the Sex Pistols at the Winterland Ballroom, where they closed the show with a remake of the Stooges classic, "No Fun." Afterward, Johnny Rotten famously kneeled down at the front of the stage and said to the audience, "Ever get the feeling you've been cheated? Goodnight."

Mothersbaugh recalled: "We saw it all go down. That was the first time we met the Sex Pistols, after their very last show. They came over to this house we were staying at [the offices of *Search And Destroy* magazine]... We'd sleep on stacks of magazines. The Sex Pistols came over and we partied all night. That was the last time I ever saw Sid Vicious and Nancy." A week later, the members of Devo were back in Akron.

▶ CHAPTER 14
SPUDBOYS VS. THE MUSIC INDUSTRY

After David Bowie announced his intentions to produce Devo, there was suddenly much interest in the Spud Boys from various record labels. However, the group decided to focus on offers from just two record companies – Warner Brothers and Virgin. The members of Devo were hesitant about signing with Warner Brothers due to a contractual provision forcing the group to work for a middleman production firm owned by David Bowie, which would receive a cut of the royalties.

Meanwhile, during a record-setting snowstorm in late-January 1978, Chris Blackwell, the head of Island Records, flew to Akron. Arriving dressed in light, tropical clothing, he was taken to the O'Neil's department store in downtown Akron to buy a much-needed winter coat. Also making the trip was Dave Robinson of Stiff Records, who had introduced the music of Devo to Blackwell. The two labels had a business relationship in which Island distributed Stiff's releases in the U.K.

The two record company heads were picked up at the airport

Richard Branson of Virgin Records.

by Akron-based songwriter and producer, Liam Sternberg, who would act as their chauffeur for a few days. Although Devo agreed to meet with Blackwell and Robinson, Jerry Casale confidently insisted that the band was about to sign with a major label.

A few days later, the members of Devo were aggressively courted by Richard Branson of Virgin Records. Mothersbaugh recalled: "Branson called me up in Akron... and said, 'Hey, you wanna come down to Jamaica?' And I looked out the window and said to myself, 'Well, it's snowing about thirty inches here.

Johnny Rotten (a.k.a. John Lydon) on a U.S. television show.

Sure, I'll come down to Jamaica.' So he flew Bob Casale and I down there to meet him and Ken Berry. We were all just sitting around in the Kingston Holiday Inn and he brought out this big stash of pot and Branson is rolling these gigantic joints on a newspaper and we're used to being in Akron where you get enough to make a paper-thin joint.... Branson said, 'I'll tell you why you're here. Johnny Rotten is down here at the hotel. He's in the next room, and there are reporters downstairs from *The New Musical Express*, *Sounds*, and *Melody Maker*. I'd like to go down to the beach right now if you're into this because

Johnny Rotten wants to join your band and I want to announce to them that Johnny Rotten is the new lead singer for Devo.'"

Seriously stoned at this point, Mothersbaugh wasn't in a clear state of mind. He recalled: "I couldn't stop laughing and told him it was the most absurd suggestion I'd ever heard. Later, Richard almost killed us. He took us to eat in the mountains and afterwards drove so fast the Jeep slid off the road and got stuck on a tree. We were in the back seat, Bob had landed on top of me and, as I looked down, it was a 100-foot drop." Many years later, Mothersbaugh realized he could have handled the proposal differently: "I've thought about it since, I've thought that would've been interesting if we would've done an album *Devo Featuring Johnny Rotten*. They just made it sound really permanent." However, Casale disagreed: "If that had happened, Devo would have probably lasted another nine months and then fallen off the face of the Earth."

Rotten wasn't the only artist that Devo turned down. Both Blondie and Iggy Pop wanted to record the group's early songs and famed composer Burt Bacharach asked to collaborate with the group. Mothersbaugh later admitted: "In retrospect, I wish we would have done every single one of them."

▶ CHAPTER 15
IN GERMANY

Agreeing to Brian Eno's offer, Devo traveled to Germany in February 1978 to record their debut album. In exchange for producing the album, Eno received a share of the profits from any subsequent record deal.

However, Jerry Casale was sidelined at a payphone at a New York City airport, arguing with his girlfriend. Missing the scheduled flight, he was a day late arriving in Germany. Unable to start the sessions without Casale, the other members of Devo were joined by Bowie, Eno and a few assorted German musicians for some informal jams – which were recorded but never released. Bowie, who was involved in several projects at the time, attended the sessions on the weekends and offered some occasional input. (Just a few months earlier, Bowie had produced Iggy Pop's well-received solo album, *Lust For Life*, at a studio in Berlin.) As for the reason behind Bowie's interest in Devo, director Julien Temple explained: "David kept up with everything, and he was especially intrigued by punk. In a way I think he felt as though he was somehow partly responsible. They were his children in a sense. He kept up, always kept up."

Casale recounted the daily routine during the sessions: "It was outside of Cologne in a place called Neunkirchen, and we were staying in this bed-and-breakfast type hotel that was a couple of steps up from a student hostel. There was no central heating, like everything in Europe. We were there in the winter under big down comforters, and we had to get up early in the morning because the schedule we were on was absurd. We'd get picked up and driven over the frozen tundra into this studio that was a converted barn in the country. The studio owner had a wife and kid, and we'd all eat breakfast with them in the morning. It was a selection of heavy meats – processed meats, sliced like Monsanto floor tiles. We didn't know what the hell it was, but they had a huge array, and this is how we started our day. It was insane."

During the sessions, the members of Devo frequently clashed with Eno and removed a great deal of instrumentation and vocal harmonies that he tried to add to the tracks. As Casale recalled: "[Eno] wanted it to be less brutal and less industrial. He wanted us to sound more melodic and pretty. That's not what we were back then, and we walked in there with a body of work we lived with and developed that was three-years-old at that point. When you're trying to establish who you are, you don't want to sound like what someone else wants you to sound like. We resisted him on the melodic stuff that sounded lush." Devo had been playing most of the album's tracks onstage for a few years and saw no reason to make drastic, last-minute changes. For the album, the group also re-recorded the four songs from their first two, self-released singles.

Not surprisingly, Eno was frustrated by the limitations

placed on him: "They were a terrifying group of people to work with because they were unwilling to experiment... I'd be sitting there at the desk, and there are EQs, echo sends, all those kinds of things, and my hand would sort of sneak up to put a bit of treatment on something, and I could feel Jerry Casale bristling behind me. It was awful! He would stand behind me all the time, then lean over and say, 'Why are you doing that?'" With the members of Devo eager to leave Germany, the sessions were quickly completed.

*   *   *   *   *   *

Before signing with either Warner Brothers or Virgin, Devo reached a short-term arrangement with Stiff Records – an independent British label that had a great deal of success with early punk and new wave acts. Stiff was licensed to distribute Devo's self-produced records throughout Europe. Dave Robinson, the label's co-owner, had found a copy of a Devo record at Bleeker Bob's Records in New York City and contacted the band to ask if they had more copies of the record. When he discovered they also had an outtake track from the Brian Eno sessions titled "Be Stiff," he became excited and wanted to release that as well. In all, Stiff would distribute three Devo singles. (Stiff would later sign two acts from Akron – Rachel Sweet and Jane Aire and the Belvederes.)

Mark Mothersbaugh recalled how the three singles achieved various levels of success around Europe: "In '77, we had five songs charted. 'Satisfaction' was No. 1 in Yugoslavia. 'Jocko Homo' was No. 4 in Scotland. 'Mongoloid' was No. 1 in France. And we didn't have a record deal." Additionally,

"Satisfaction" peaked at No. 41 on the British charts.

After the completion of their sessions in Germany with Brian Eno, Devo was invited by Stiff Records to play a few shows in England. Attending one of these performances was an old friend from Akron – Chrissie Hynde. At one venue, the band played inside a square, metal cage, which was surrounded by audience members.

During the short tour, Mothersbaugh recalled that Devo was not embraced by the London punk scene: "The punk bands decided we weren't punks. They weren't about anarchy, they were conformist and anti-intellectual and angry in a nasty way. So they'd come and see us and laugh and spit at us, the pale, punk scientists from America. But we didn't care. One writer from *Melody Maker* really went after us. He insinuated his way on to our tour bus, then wrote down everything we said and did but in as snarky a way as possible, like, 'Jerry turned his head like a squirrel' or 'he tittered like a piglet.' Our British success made Americans prick up their ears." At around the same time, fellow Akronite Chrissie Hynde was also having some trouble integrating into the emerging British punk scene, which she attributed to her outsider status as an American.

While in England, Devo received an improved offer from Richard Branson of Virgin Records and signed a contract to release the group's music in Europe. Upon learning the news, Warner Brothers sued both Branson and Devo in a British court. Warner claimed they had the legal right to the group's debut album after financing some of the costs associated with the recording sessions in Germany. Faced with Warner Brother's combative team of lawyers, the members of Devo knew they had to quickly settle the matter. Eventually, the two labels worked out an agreement that invalidated the earlier contract Devo had signed and gave Virgin the right to release the group's material in Europe, with Warner claiming most of the rest of the world. The deal was nearly identical to what Devo had proposed to Warner Brothers a few months earlier but was far less lucrative for the band.

Additionally, Devo agreed to take a lower royalty rate in order to retain creative control of the group's album artwork, music and merchandising. Unfortunately, the group agreed to an unfavorable publishing deal that would result in millions of dollars in lost earnings over the next several decades. Years later, Mothersbaugh would lament signing the original deal with Branson: "We made a mistake by trusting him."

In late-June 1978, Devo made a return trip to England to perform for their largest audience to date. Appearing at the prestigious Knebworth Festival, just north of London, Devo took the stage following a solid performance by an upstart American band, Tom Petty and the Heartbreakers. Branson believed it would be a good idea to add Devo to the lineup.

Unfortunately, Devo's appearance was a disaster. From the onset, the group was met with a widespread barrage of mud and bottles as well as verbal abuse from the overtly hostile crowd. The old guard, long-haired hippies in the audience were not amused by the new wave of pop music and made their displeasure known. While hundreds of projectiles were hurled in the direction of the stage, most landed on other concertgoers, which had the secondary effect of sparking a large number of brawls.

Mark Mothersbaugh recalled: "We'd only played small clubs before, so we didn't even have a crew. We set up our gear wearing blue work gear, ran to change into our yellow stage suits to perform, then changed into the blue overalls again to take the equipment down."

▶ CHAPTER 16
ARE WE NOT MEN?

Nearly six-months after it was recorded, the much-awaited album, *Q: Are We Not Men? A: We Are Devo!*, was released on August 28, 1978. Even the album's artwork created some headaches for the band. The front cover featured a cartoon drawing of professional golfer Chi Chi Rodriguez that was based on an image from a package of golf balls, which Casale had discovered while perusing the close-out aisle at a department store in Akron. Warner Brothers refused to release the original cover featuring the unaltered image unless the band got permission from the golfer, which he eventually gave. However, due to the delay is securing his consent, Warner Brothers chose to issue the album with an altered image of Rodriguez. (Ironically, he was legendary for turning down sponsorship deals.)

There was another potential legal problem. One of the album's highlights was a deconstructed rendition of the Rolling Stones classic, "(I Can't Get No) Satisfaction." Due to the fact that the song was unlike the original version and could be

Mick Jagger, right, with the Rolling Stones.

considered a derivative musical piece, Warner Brothers forced Devo to secure permission from one of the song's composers, Mick Jagger.

Arriving in Manhattan, Devo played their rendition of the song for Jagger on a portable cassette player. Casale recalled that after thirty-seconds of silence, Jagger "suddenly stood up and started dancing around on this Afghan rug in front of the fireplace, the sort of rooster-man dance he used to do, and saying, 'I like it, I like it.' Mark and I lit up, big smiles on our faces, like in *Wayne's World*: 'We're not worthy!' To see your icon that you grew up admiring, that you had seen in concert, dancing around like Mick Jagger being Mick Jagger. It was unbelievable."

However, Jerry Casale later lamented: "People thought it was a parody and were insulted by it. We weren't doing a parody; we were playing homage to one of the greatest rock 'n' roll songs ever written, and I remember that Jann Wenner (publisher of *Rolling Stone* magazine), when he heard it, he was truly offended."

Another track, "Come Back Jonee" – which was a reference to John F. Kennedy – became a fan favorite. A video for the song, which cost $7,500, was filmed at the Roxy Theatre in Los Angeles. In the video, the over-exuberant fans stormed the stage. The video was shot by Chuck Statler, who would continue to work with the group until 1982. He would also oversee a number of other well-known MTV videos for artists such as the Cars, Elvis Costello, Madness and Nick Lowe.

Two other tracks on the album were ahead of their time and would have easily been radio hits in the 1980s – "Gut Feeling," which had a hard-driving, two-minute intro; and the frenetic "Uncontrollable Urge," which featured Brian Eno on backing vocals. The latter song's accompanying robotic dance was created by the band in the basement of a house in Akron's Highland Square neighborhood.

During a meeting with Warner Brothers, Devo was apprised of the label's plans for promoting the album. Mothersbaugh recalled: "One guy goes, 'Here's the marketing plan for your music: We're going to put life-size cut-outs of you in every major record store in the country.' And then he just leaned back and smiled and the other guys tipped their coffee cups. We looked around. That was it. We said, 'How much will that cost?' $5,000. 'Can we have that money to make a film instead?' They were like, 'A film? What can we do with a film?' We took the $5,000 and made the 'Satisfaction' video, and they indeed had no idea what to do with it."

The bulk of the video was filmed on the stage of the Akron

Civic Theater. Additionally, some of the scenes were shot inside a car driven by Robert Mothersbaugh Sr. through the parking lot of the State Road Shopping Center in Cuyahoga Falls and featured Mark Mothersbaugh trying to make out with his date in the backseat. However, the clip's most memorable scene featured a contorting punk rocker named Spazz Attack (real name Craig Allen Rothwell), who performed a series of forward flips onto his back. He was discovered by the members of Devo on the dance floor of a Los Angeles nightclub. In the video's most controversial scene, Mothersbaugh's Booji Boy character receives an electric shock after sticking a metal fork into a toaster. As a result, the video was banned by both the BBC in Britain and the NBC television program, *Midnight Special*.

Although Devo's debut album received mixed reviews in the rock press, the group's unique sound and public image attracted much attention. A *Rolling Stone* reviewer described the album as "a brittle, small masterpiece of Seventies pop irony, but its shriveling, ice-cold absurdism might not define the Seventies as much as jump the gun on the Eighties."

While the album peaked at an impressive #12 in the U.K., it managed to reach just #72 in the U.S. At the end of the year, the album was ranked at #20 on *The Village Voice's* 1978 Jazz & Pop poll. Casale later recalled: "It was a wonderful gulp of water after years in the desert where we were either hated and ignored or laughed at, to finally get some kind of positive feedback; that what you had believed is possible had a core of validity." Remarkably, it would take 23-years for *Q: Are We Not Men* to be certified Gold in the U.S., marking the sales of 500,000 copies.

Meanwhile, Devo continued to open their shows by projecting their videos onto a white bed sheet before taking the stage. Mothersbaugh recalled: "It's like a scientific experiment. We can always tell [the moment] when Booji Boy sticks his fork in the toaster, and we know the general level of the crowd by how many howls and low, guttural noises there are, compared to appreciative laughter and clapping."

Now spreading the Spud Boy philosophy to the masses, Casale told a reporter during this period: "We're all Devo. Devo is self-contradictory and absurd, and yet definitely human. It's a technique for dissecting everything you see, every piece of information. It's like a goo, an amoeba, a blob. It's the alien approach. Take yourself out of it and be in it at the same time."

▶ CHAPTER 17
LEAVING AKRON

The members of Devo realized it was necessary to relocate from post-industrial Akron to the flourishing metropolis of Los Angeles. After quickly building a solid fanbase on the West Coast, the decision made financial sense. In the fall of 1978, Devo launched a U.S. tour beginning with a show at the Starwood. *Rolling Stone* reported: "They played to a sell-out crowd that included Bruce Springsteen, Ron Wood, Todd Rundgren, David Blue and Leonard Cohen. Asked his opinion of the band, Cohen replied, 'It's nice to see an act whose audience can't relate to them.'"

In a short period of time, Devo had managed to become a lightning rod of controversy in popular culture. Casale later recalled: "If you liked Devo, it was either a badge of courage or a prison stamp. We were the original nerd band when rock was supposed to be macho. Now it's okay to be a nerdy rocker; then – it got you beat up."

Meanwhile, Devo had hired Elliot Roberts as their new manager, only after he offered the group a coveted slot on *Saturday Night Live*. (Roberts promised *SNL* a future appearance by Neil Young if Devo was given a slot on the show.) As the musical guests on October 14, 1978, Devo unleashed a strong rendition of "Jocko Homo" and a herky-jerky, robotic version of "(I Can't Get No) Satisfaction" on a stage that was covered with a sheet of black plastic. (Coincidentally, the Rolling Stones had appeared on *SNL* the previous week and had unexpectedly also performed "(I Can't Get No) Satisfaction.")

Dressed in their signature yellow industrial suits and inverted 3-D glasses, the members of Devo were unlike any previous musical act on the show. While most viewers were unnerved by the irreverent, electronic rendition of the rock standard, a significant number of music aficionados were mesmerized.

Just three-days later, Devo played a pair of sold-out shows at the 400-seat Bottom Line nightclub in New York, which attracted many curious movers and shakers from the entertainment industry. (During the first show, Casale placed a television on the front of the stage so that the New York crowd could watch the final game of the World Series, in which the Yankees defeated the Dodgers.) Several weeks later, Devo was pictured on the cover of *New York Rocker* magazine, with the caption, "Devo: Bigger Than Christmas?"

Casale recalled how all of a sudden, the members of the band were treated as celebrities: "There were throngs of people outside your hotel. You couldn't go to a restaurant – it was amazing."

Staying on the road for the next three-months, Devo performed at the Cleveland Agora on October 30. A reviewer wrote: "The band's anthem, 'Jocko Homo,' drew the wildest response of the evening." One of the opening acts was the Akron new wave trio, Chi-Pig.

In mid-November, Devo spent three-weeks touring Europe, beginning with a show in Germany. European audiences – which had already been exposed to the electronic dance music of Kraftwerk – welcomed the Spud Boys from Akron. Casale admitted: "Of course, we came to know about Kraftwerk. We didn't know about them when we started out. But it was like, 'Oh, there's people kind of doing us.' Except we were different. We might have been Kraftwerk from the waist up, but we were Elvis from the waist down."

On January 4, 1979, Devo took the stage at the Akron Civic Theater. Tickets were $6 in advance and $7 on the day of the show. This would mark the group's last performance in the Rubber City for nearly thirty-years. If Akronites wanted to see the band, they would have to travel elsewhere for the opportunity.

Clearly, Devo still couldn't gain any respect from music fans in Northeastern Ohio. In February, Devo was the recipient of two unflattering awards in a poll conducted by radio powerhouse WMMS and *The Cleveland Plain Dealer*. The paper reported: "Devo was voted the Worst New Artist, far ahead of all competition. And its album, *Q: Are We Not Men? We Are Devo!* was named the Worst Album." It wasn't that the residents of Akron and Cleveland disliked new wave – they just didn't embrace Devo. The Cars – a new wave act that included two former Clevelanders, Ric Ocasek and Benjamin Orr – were voted Best New Artist.

Meanwhile, after his dismissal as Devo's manager, former member Bob Lewis demanded financial compensation for his role in the creation of the group and its central doctrine. In response, the other members of Devo sued in a Los Angeles Superior Court, asking for a declaratory judgment against Lewis. Filing a separate suit in Ohio, Lewis came to court with reams of evidence to document his claims. After a three-year battle, the matter was subsequently settled in Lewis' favor for an undisclosed sum. (Several years earlier, Robert Mothersbaugh Sr. had offered to manage the group and was heartbroken when his sons turned him down.)

▶ CHAPTER 18
THE AKRON SOUND

Almost overnight, Akron lost most of its economic cornerstones as the city was in the midst of a major downturn. Over a several-year period ending in 1982, all of Akron's big rubber factories stopped producing passenger tires. As writer Russ Musarra observed: "Employment in Akron rubber companies, once at 60,000, was 28,453 in 1976 after a four-month strike, longest in the industry's history. By 1982, plant closings had reduced employment to 17,366."

The huge loss in the number of good-paying factory jobs would also devastate other businesses in the city. Downtown's two majestic department stores – Polsky's and O'Neil's – would soon shutter their doors. Even the city's fabled downtown record store, Edfred's, closed down in 1978 after 64-years in business.

From this post-industrial landscape of abandoned factories all across the Midwest, a new term emerged – the Rust Belt. Local musician Brad Warner recalled: "One of my clearest memories of Akron from when I used to go there with my dad from the suburbs where we lived is the smell. As soon as you

Abandoned tire factory in Akron.

crossed the city limits, it was like you were breathing the fumes of a million tires. The perpetually cloudy skies turned a shade grayer from the tons of smoke Firestone, Goodyear, Goodrich and Seiberling constantly pumped into the air. By the time I graduated high school in 1982, that smell was already a thing of the past."

Likewise, LeBron James said of his hometown: "If you went high up on North Hill in the 1980s, you could tell that life was not like it once was: the obsolete smokestacks in the distance, the downtown felt so tired and weary. I won't deny it – there was something painful about all of that."

Dan Auerbach of the Black Keys observed: "It's kind of a strange little town. It's got all these ghosts of the past lurking around every corner, these giant buildings, old mansions everywhere. Empty factory buildings. Turn of the century Akron was just poppin' like crazy. Some of the richest people in North America were living there and had mansions. And then all of that went away!"

Downtown Akron resembled a ghost town in the evenings after office and government workers went home for the day. During this period, adventurous locals would explore a pair of once-thriving but boarded-up downtown buildings, the Portage Hotel and the grain silos inside the former Quaker Oats factory.

Although the local economy was decaying and the region's population was shrinking, there was still a strong art and music scene. And in the wake of Devo's success, there was a creative buzz in the local nightclubs as an increasing number of bands performed original music. The movement was soon dubbed the Akron Sound. Local musician Ralph Carney of Tin Huey observed: "I think it was all the rubber dust we inhaled. I think there are similar scenes in many industrial towns like Detroit but in Akron, there definitely was an unusual amount of weird bands. When you're in a place like Akron, you make up your own reality of what you want to play."

Meanwhile, after the closure of the Crypt, the local new wave and punk scene soon relocated to a downtown Akron nightclub, the Bank. The club was nestled inside a former bank branch on the ground floor of the crumbling Anthony Wayne Hotel, which was built in 1916. The club's owner – a local attorney in his 50s – used the bank's steel vault to store liquor.

Initially operating as a jazz club, the venue struggled to stay open. Out of economic necessity, the owner agreed to book punk and new wave acts after a few of the displaced bands from the Crypt inquired about performing at the club. What started as a two-night-per-week experiment was quickly expanded. While jazz artists failed to attract paying customers, rock acts

The Bank nightclub in downtown Akron.

packed the club.

The Bank was also the inspiration for a Hollywood film, *Light Of Day*, which starred Joan Jett and Michael J. Fox as members of a fictional Cleveland bar band. The screenplay was written by director Paul Schrader and was loosely based on the Cleveland rock band, the Generators.

The initial idea for the film came to Schrader after a visit to the Bank. Akron new wave singer Nick Nicholis recalled: "[Schrader] was having me take him around one night when we went to see Klaus Nomi, who was this really weird opera singer guy playing the Bank. Nomi was on stage and the place was packed. We were on the balcony just looking down on the stage at this guy performing in a tutu, all these strange lights were shining everywhere, a parachute was draped from the ceiling and 500 people were crammed in there dancing. It was really amazing – like being in a Fellini movie. We could've been in Japan, Germany, New York or anywhere that night." Nomi, who spent a few weeks in Akron, had been invited to play at the Bank by members of the Akron new wave band Chi-Pig, after playing a gig in New York City.

In addition to the Crypt and the Bank, Akron's new wave acts frequently performed in Kent, just twenty-minutes east of downtown Akron, at J.B.'s, Mothers Junction, the Robin Hood and the Rathskeller. J.B.'s, the most legendary of these venues, had been a proving ground for up-and-coming local rock acts like the James Gang, the Raspberries and Glass Harp since the mid-1960s.

Meanwhile, Nicholis launched his own label, Clone Records. In 1977, he released the album, *From Akron*, which featured one side by Nicholis' own band, the Bizarros, and the Rubber City Rebels on the other. The son of a tire factory worker, Nicholis took his group's name from a Superman comic book. Formed by students at the University of Akron, the Bizarros were not performing the kind of mainstream rock their classmates heard on local commercial radio. (Meanwhile, the university's campus radio station, WZIP, began playing new wave music in 1980 on a full-time basis.)

Wanting to promote the city's thriving music scene, Nicholis sent a copy of *From Akron* to notable New York City-based

Nick Nicholis of the Bizarros.

music critic, Robert Christgau. At the same time, Chris Butler of Tin Huey regularly mailed letters to Christgau, chastising him for ignoring the city's many talented acts.

Finally, Christgau penned an article for *The Village Voice*, which was headlined, "A New Wave Rolls Out Of Akron." In the lengthy piece, he wrote: "When I visited Ohio in early March, the Devo musicians were touring England. But I was able to meet with Bob Lewis, their quasi-manager and longtime conceptual collaborator, in a cheap, comfortable double apartment maintained by two women who introduced themselves as Susan Devo and Bobbie Devo. Like so much new wave, the Devo idea – sci-fi technological love-hate enriched by scatological slapstick and relentless oxymoron – reinterprets and adapts counterculture perceptions rather than reducing them to toothless cliches. So it wasn't surprising to find that the band's headquarters felt like a commune, or to hear Bobbie refer to the Devo 'community.' Their manifestos of five or six years ago – took an anti-android tone, favoring what Lewis called 'that transcendent state most fully engendered by Fred Flintstone – the technologically sophisticated cave-man.'"

Around this time, Devo was asked by a reporter from Liverpool to describe the city of Akron. When Mark Mothersbaugh replied, "It's a lot like Liverpool," the journalist misinterpreted the statement to mean that the Rubber City was a rock mecca with a booming musical scene. Consequently, the British music press – led by *Melody Maker* – jumped on the comment and suddenly Akron was placed on a new wave pedestal as the "new Liverpool."

Meanwhile, Nicholis recalled how the rock press subsequently converged on the Rubber City: "A lot of people came here. Bob Christgau from *The Village Voice* stayed at my house while he did this huge story on Akron, and writers from places like *Trouser Press* and *New York Rocker* were always asking us to take them places." After Christgau compared the Bizarros to the avant-garde rockers Velvet Underground – which was one of Nicholis' major influences – the Bizarros were signed by the Mercury subsidiary, Blank Records. (The same label had already signed another area band, Pere Ubu.)

In June 1978, Christgau agreed to return to the area and

Rachel Sweet on a U.K. tour in 1978.

attend a showcase of Akron new wave bands at J.B.'s in Kent. One of the bands, Tin Huey, would soon sign with Warner Brothers.

In July, Devo appeared on the cover of the British rock publication, *Sounds*. Above a photo of the band, the magazine announced a contest: "Win a Trip to Akron!" The *lucky* winner was promised a tour of a Firestone tire plant. (Just five-months later, Phil Lynott of Thin Lizzy would appear on the cover of the same magazine dressed like a member of Devo.)

Also in 1978, the premier U.K. punk label, Stiff Records, agreed to issue a collection of tracks by a variety of Akron new wave acts. After the label's co-owner, Dave Robinson, had failed to sign Devo during his visit to Akron, he stuck around for a week and met a number of other emerging acts. After returning to England, Robinson was convinced by his friend, Chrissie Hynde, that he should issue the album.

The Akron Compilation was assembled with the aid of local musician Liam Sternberg – who was classically trained at the University of Akron – and Chris Butler. With Devo refusing to contribute any material, Sternberg and Butler wrote seven of the fourteen songs on the project and *invented* some of the Akron bands. Released in June, the album featured a scratch-and-sniff tire-scented cover. It was not a strong seller.

Soon after, Sternberg traveled to London, where he would produce an album by one of the acts on *The Akron Compilation*, Rachel Sweet. Later, Sternberg would write the chart-topping Bangles' hit, "Walk Like An Egyptian." After completing a demo version of "Egyptian" with Marti Jones providing the lead vocals, Sternberg initially offered the song to Toni Basil, who turned it down. Sternberg, who later married rock journalist Silvie Simmons, also wrote "They Don't Know," a hit for Tracey Ullman, and the theme for the Fox television series, *21 Jump Street*.

More attention to the Akron Sound came after the release of a pair of multi-artist sampler albums issued by Clone Records, *Bowling Balls From Hell, Vols. 1 & 2*. One of the featured artists, Hurricane Bob, was actually Devo co-founder Bob Lewis. Debbie Smith of Chi-Pig recalled: "The exposure was a great boost for everyone's career. It gave us confidence, maybe even a little cockiness. It was exciting to feel like we were on the cutting edge, which is not necessarily a familiar feeling for Akron musicians."

Meanwhile, the Rubber City Rebels were signed by Sire Records. But due to a series of unfortunate events – including their manager's insistence on recording the project in a Los Angeles studio – the group was dropped by the label. By year's end, the group splintered into two camps. Disheartened by the Los Angeles music scene, members Mike Hammer and Donnie Damage returned to Akron and formed the self-described "power-pop" group, Hammer Damage, along with Scott Winkler and George Cabaniss. Aside from performing original material, Hammer Damage also relied on an assortment of Rubber City Rebels songs. Cabaniss later left to join the Dead Boys.

Later, the Rubber City Rebels were befriended by members of an emerging band, the Knack. With the aid of the group's singer, Doug Fieger, the Akron act was signed to Capitol Records. In 1980, the Rubber City Rebels issued a self-titled album, which Fieger produced. But while the Knack's explosive debut disc would sell six-million copies in the U.S., the Rebels' album was ignored.

Similarly, Tin Huey also failed to elicit interest. Following the poor sales of 1979's *Contents Dislodged During Shipment*, Warner Brothers renegotiated Tin Huey's contract and paid the band $50,000 to *not* record a scheduled second album. The group disbanded later that year. Meanwhile, Tin Huey member Ralph Carney moved to Woodstock, New York. He would work with the B-52's until 1984, when the group decided it no longer needed horn players. In 1985, he joined Tom Waits' backing band. Carney's nephew, Patrick Carney, would later form the Black Keys.

Meanwhile, Chris Butler of Tin Huey would have greater success with his informal side-project – the Waitresses. The inspiration for the group's biggest hit, "I Know What Boys Like," came from a cramped and noisy watering hole in Akron's Highland Square district. As Butler explained in the book, *Mad World*, he enlisted a friend to provide the lead vocal on what was intended as a demo recording: "I liked Patty Donahue's deadpan delivery. She was a girl about town, and she was a firecracker and a fun person.... I was like, 'Just do that thing where the guy comes up to you at the bar who you don't want to do the deal with,' and she goes, 'Oh yeah, I know how to do that.'"

Butler recalled how the Waitresses found some unexpected success: "Tin Huey had done very well in New York. It was the only place we had done well. I had that [demo] version of 'I Know What Boys Like,' and I played it to a couple of people, and they thought it was a hit. This guy named Mark Kamins, who was a DJ at Danceteria, flipped over it. He played it a couple times one night, then the next day he took it up to Island Records and... they wanted to sign it. They said, 'Where's the band?' I lied and said, 'They're back in Ohio.'" Needing a B-side for a single, Butler brought Patty Donahue to New York and asked a few friends to appear on the quickly organized sessions. In the coming years, "I Know What Boys Like" became a new wave standard. The group also had success with the perennial holiday classic, "Christmas Wrapping," and recorded the theme of the television series, *Square Pegs*.

Other notable Akron Sound acts from this period included Unit 5, Human Switchboard, the F-Models, the Action and Jane Aire & The Belvederes.

Another act, the Cramps, was formed in Akron's Highland Square neighborhood by Erick Purkhiser and Kristy Wallace – better known by their stage names, Lux Interior and Poison Ivy. Purkhiser recalled: "It was so great when we started going to rock shows together.... In those days, the audience was wilder than the bands, and Ivy was always one of the wildest. So it wasn't much of a jump for us to become a band. We were both collecting old 45s from junk stores, and we just thought that maybe we could do the same thing with rockabilly that the Stones and Pretty Things did with R&B in the '60s. We just had to learn how to play songs."

Realizing that New York City offered far better opportunities for their offbeat brand of music, the Cramps left Akron. Poison Ivy admitted, "We were arrogant enough to think, 'Let's move to New York and play at CBGB.'" After arriving in the Big Apple, she observed: "For some reason there was a ton of people from Ohio who were in New York. And none of them knew each other in New York."

Punk rock also thrived in Akron during this period. Brad Warner, a member of Zero Defex, recalled: "A lot of other hardcore scenes were characterized by violence. But not ours. For example, there was a rule at the shows we set up that people who wore spikes were not allowed to slam dance. Spiked wristbands and collars were, of course, a major part of punk fashion. As was full-contact slam dancing in which people careened about the dance floor like whirling dervishes and smashed into each other like dodgem cars. Jimi Imij and Vince Rancid, who more or less ran the shows in those days, would police the audience for people wearing spikes and make those folks take them off before allowing them on the dance floor.

Some people protested; apparently one guy had to be held down on the ground and forced to remove his wristband. But most of us were glad to comply. Although the scene ended, its ideals have been retained by most of those who participated." (Warner later produced the 2007 film, *Cleveland Screaming*, which documented the Northeastern Ohio punk scenes. Meanwhile, Jimi Imij later became an archivist of the Akron music scene.)

Mike Purkhiser – the guitarist of the Action and the brother of the Cramps' Lux Interior – wondered if there really was a unified Akron Sound; he said at the time: "You can tell the difference between our music and, say, Chi-Pig or Hammer Damage or any of the others. We all have our own sound. But there was a common denominator. I think it's the creativity, the originality we're all after.... I think we're all tired of the same old thing and that we all want to create something new. That's something a lot of people don't understand. We're not trying to be weird just to be weird. We're trying to create a scene, an excitement that hasn't existed in music for a long time."

Eventually, the Akron Sound reached its end in the early-1980s, ironically just as new wave was embraced by mainstream America. Years later, Rod Firestone of the Rubber City Rebels stated: "I doubt if the locals are aware of how far and wide is the Akron legend. The Rebels can go to... Tokyo and play to sellout crowds, Those kinds know all the Akron bands and have all the records. Some musicians in Tokyo just told me that they hope to go to Akron someday. I would like to see [Akron-raised director Jim] Jarmusch make that movie. Japanese guy comes all the way from Japan. Gets off bus. Then what? There's not exactly an East Village he can go to. I guess he could go to Luigi's and say 'Donnie Damage ate here.'"

Local musician Jon Mosey summed up the fate of the bands who found fame and success as part of the Akron Sound: "All of a sudden they were big names – for a minute. And then all of a sudden they're all back in Akron."

As for Akron's pioneering new wave clubs, the Crypt was later bulldozed and paved over. The site is now a car dealership. The Bank suffered a similar fate and was demolished to make way for a $40 million, minor-league baseball stadium. Meanwhile, J.B.'s in Kent went through numerous changes in ownership and no longer hosts live music.

▶ CHAPTER 19
DEVO & NEIL YOUNG

During Devo's first run of shows in San Francisco, the group came to the attention of Neil Young. After actor Dean Stockwell had played Young a cassette of Devo's early recordings, the plaid-shirt-wearing classic rocker was instantly hooked. Attending a Devo performance, Young asked the group to appear in his avant-garde film, *Human Highway*. Although production began in 1978, the film would not be completed until 1982 at a cost of $3 million, which Young personally funded.

Young later described the oddball film: "It was sort of [a] day-in-the-life concept, all taking place in one day, just a regular day, the day the earth suddenly ended in a world war. It was a comedy. Every day we began with shooting the script we had come up with the night before. What a blast!"

Jerry Casale said of Young: "He's really a strange and complicated guy. And really tense. Very smart and very conflicted. We thought, 'Ho ho ho, the grandfather of granola rock wants to meet us.' But I loved his music.... He said, 'You decide what you want to do,' so we decided we were waste

Neil Young, right, and Paul McCartney in Los Angeles.

workers pissed off about our job.... They built a whole set with a loading dock and got a truck in there. It was the only time in years that I got to use 35mm film."

In the film, Young wanted the members of Devo to appear as characters in his nightmare, which he named "Nuclear Garbagepersons." Driving a waste disposal truck, the members of the group dumped toxic waste into a pristine river. Casale recalled interacting with the actors on the set of the film: "We met Dennis Hopper and Dean Stockwell at the low point in their lives. They were so high and screwed up on the set everyday, and pulling pranks, and just being anarchists and causing problems!"

The film opened with Mark Mothersbaugh – in his masked Booji Boy persona – giving an oddball, spoken rendition of the Bob Dylan classic, "Blowin' In The Wind." Additionally, Devo performed the songs, "Come Back Jonee" and a reworked rendition of an old folk standard first made popular by the Carter Family in 1930, "It Takes A Worried Man" (also known as "Worried Man Blues").

In another scene, which was filmed inside Different Fur Studios in San Francisco, Devo was joined by Young for a duet of "Hey Hey, My My (Into The Black)." Booji Boy provided the lead vocals while sitting in a borrowed crib: "There's a scene where I'm wearing a rubber mask and diapers, and sitting in a playpen, and halfway through the song Neil smashes the playpen up with the guitar. Which really wasn't something we'd rehearsed."

Casale later recalled: "That was just such an amazing time – so chaotic and revolutionary and unexpected. I thought, 'Why would Neil Young like Devo?' I thought I knew him. And then I realized I didn't. We met him, and he was so much more than what I thought. He was very funny, smart and hip. And it made sense. In other words, why should I put him in a corner just because of the style of his music? We didn't like to be put in a corner. He was open to everything."

As the result of his association with Devo, an inspired Neil Young shocked his longtime fans and upset his record company when he abandoned his classic rock roots and released a new wave album in 1983, *Trans*.

▶ CHAPTER 20
DUTY NOW FOR THE FUTURE

In September 1978, Devo began working on their second album, *Duty Now For The Future*. Producer Ken Scott recalled his initial reaction to the group's music: "I [had] started to use a studio in North Hollywood named Chateau Recorders. The second engineer at Chateau Recorders, a guy named Chris Gregg, was from the Midwest and was always raving about this band from Ohio who thought the world was falling apart and believed in something called 'de-evolution.' As a result, they called their band Devo. He brought in some of their garage tapes and I must say, I did not get it at all. 'That sounds atrocious,' I remember telling him after a quick listen. A short time after that, their first album came out and they happened to be appearing on *Saturday Night Live* on an evening when I was off. I thought, 'OK, this is the band that Chris was telling me about. Let me check them out.' When I saw them, I suddenly got it. I loved them. A while later I received a phone call from Devo's management company about meeting with me and talking about doing their next album. My understanding is that they liked what I'd done with Bowie, and that's what brought us together." In addition to Bowie, Scott had also produced both Elton John and Supertramp, and had engineered two albums for the Beatles.

Released in July 1979, *Duty Now For The Future* had an unusual front cover that sported nearly three-dozen bar codes. Most of the tracks had been written before the release of the group's first album. Devo had been regularly performing the songs onstage for a few years and had a good grasp of how they should sound on record. However, Mothersbaugh announced during the sessions that he wanted to drop some of the songs and write new material. Unfortunately, some of the newer tracks weren't up to par.

The album's first single, "The Day My Baby Gave Me A Surprize," was ignored by radio. (The crying baby in the song's music video was Bob 1's oldest daughter.) Instead, the project was highlighted by the second single, a remake of the 1960s pop standard, "Secret Agent Man." (Devo had recorded an earlier version of the track in 1974.) In the music video – which cost $50,000 – Jerry Casale made a rare appearance as his early stage character, Chinaman. Also appearing in the video was Toni Basil, who portrayed Soo Bawlz, the girlfriend of Chinaman.

Another track, the medley of "Smart Patrol"/"Mr. DNA," quickly became a fan favorite at Devo shows. And an instrumental track, "Corporate Anthem Theme," was inspired by the 1975 science-fiction film, *Rollerball*. As a joke, Mothersbaugh had sent an altered version of the song – with mocking lyrics – to Idi Amin, the murderous president of Uganda.

Reviews for the album were mixed. At *Rolling Stone*

magazine, notable writer Dave Marsh wasn't impressed: "Most of the concepts on their second album... have been recycled from Frank Zappa, the Yardbirds and other Sixties avant-gardists – and the handful of original notions they do try to express are mostly lame or fraudulent." Casale, who was also unhappy with the project, later admitted: "I think, if anything, that album proves that we weren't up to a big plan. Because if we had been we wouldn't have made that album, would we?"

At the end of 1979, Casale told a reporter that the group's debut album, *Q: Are We Not Men?* had sold "just under 200,000 in the U.S., just under 120,000 in Europe, and 50,000 in Canada. And the only reason that's good is because there was very little to zero airplay. Now we're getting more airplay and that's the important thing. The audience is there."

Mothersbaugh described Devo's relationship with their label at the time: "We were critical darlings with no airplay, basically. Warners was very disappointed with the second record... because coming off of the explosion of the first record, going on *Saturday Night Live* and having a national platform, they were seeing dollar signs. And it didn't happen."

Meanwhile, during the final dates of their *Duty Now For The Future* tour, the members of Devo decided to transform themselves into their own opening act – a soft-rock pop group. Taking the stage as Dove (an anagram of Devo), Mothersbaugh and his bandmates wore olive-green leisure suits, lime-green polyester shirts and plastic bankers visors. Not surprisingly, Dove was poorly received by audiences. Dove also made an appearance in the 1981 comedy film, *Pray TV*.

* * * * * *

During this period, Devo introduced their signature red energy domes, which were often mocked in the press as upside-down flower pots. However, the group's striking headwear caught the attention of the American public and would come to symbolize both Devo as well as the entire new wave era.

Jerry Casale, who came up with the design, was originally inspired by the shape of the white, art deco, crystal lights he had admired on the ceiling of his Catholic school in Kent, St. Patrick's. He was also influenced by a comic strip: "The hats came from a *Nancy* cartoon with what were called cancellator helmets. Nancy would put one on, and she'd be unable to hear the outside world. She got Sluggo and everyone into these cancellator helmets. It was like a form of meditation; they weren't upset anymore because they couldn't hear people talking to them. The way they were drawn looked like ziggerauts from the Mayans or Aztecs, and I thought it was great.... We put hat liners inside and called them energy domes."

Meanwhile, Devo discovered how to create a new income stream. After learning that unauthorized third parties were selling bootleg Devo products, the group launched its own merchandising arm, Club Devo, to sell various items, including posters, rubber suits, postcards, turtlenecks, and the group's signature energy domes. When a rock critic accused the band of "turning into a punk version of Kiss," Casale replied, "Yeah, I've heard that before. I've also heard we were a Kiss for college students, and I thought and said, 'Hmm, that's not so bad what that implies." Meanwhile, there was a change in the group's dynamics as soundman and longtime Devo insider Ed Barger was unceremoniously dismissed by the group after an infamous gig in Long Beach, California.

▶ CHAPTER 21
FREEDOM OF CHOICE

In October 1979, Devo began working on their third album. Under threat from Warner Brothers, Devo adjusted their sound. However, unlike their first two albums, the group labored to come up with new material. In the end, the resulting tracks were danceable, more mainstream and solidly in the new wave camp.

Jerry Casale recalled: "We were starting to explore and experiment in a new direction. We had made some basic decisions that I was going to play bass on a mini-Moog [synthesizer], for instance. And we were going to do some twisted version of Devo R&B. In other words, rhythm and blues would be a starting point for inspiration, since Bob Mothersbaugh and I particularly loved all of that growing up." This was the first Devo album that didn't feature songs written in Akron.

Robert Margouleff, who co-produced and co-engineered the album, recalled meeting the band: "I was sitting in the front office at the Record Plant [in Los Angeles] when I first set eyes on Devo. A Volkswagen with dark windows pulled into the parking lot and all of them got out wearing jumpsuits, black rubber boots, red helmets, tanks attached to the helmets, and hoses from the tanks running up their noses. Everyone in the studio was completely nonplussed but we didn't show it; this was the Record Plant, so any freak was alright with us. Anyway, Devo knew my work with Stevie Wonder, and when they came into the building they were very up-front, asking me if I'd be interested in working with them on the production of *Freedom Of Choice*. Having finished with Stevie, I was looking for interesting things to do, and since Devo's music related to my roots in electronica it seemed like a natural match."

The members of Devo came prepared for the sessions. As Margouleff recalled: "You have to understand that Mark and Jerry are very smart and extremely talented, and so my job was really just to help channel that and bring a different point of view to the mix, which I did." With the technology of music quickly evolving, former Devo member Jim Mothersbaugh would occasionally join his former bandmates in the studio to provide some expertise.

The album, *Freedom Of Choice*, was released on May 16, 1980. For the front cover, the members of Devo wore silver-hued naugahyde suits and red energy domes. Most reviewers praised the album, including Robert Christgau, who gave it a B+ and wrote: "If they ever teach a rhythm box to get funky, a Mothersbaugh will be there to plug it in." However, a critic at *Newsday* viciously attacked the project and the band: "As it turns out, Devo was a bunch of marvelous cons. The band's third album, *Freedom Of Choice*, proves the quartet to be uninventive hacks who've taken their gimmick as far as it can go. From the cultural parody of the first album, they've descended into terminal self-parody."

On May 23, Devo was the featured musical act on the ABC series, *Fridays*, which was launched as an alternative to the hugely popular NBC show, *Saturday Night Live*. Devo performed two songs, "Girl U Want" and "Gates Of Steel." Over the next two-years, Devo would make two more appearances on *Fridays*.

Although Warner Brothers had high hopes for the album's first single, "Girl U Want," it was ignored by radio and flopped on the charts. The song's music video featured the members of Devo in purple energy domes. For a second single, Warner Brothers was planning to issue "Freedom Of Choice" – which was inspired by a Roman fable by Phaedrus. Casale explained, "We loved that song very much when we were creating it. It was about how people were throwing away their freedom of choice into meaningless choices like between Pepsi and Coke, or pink fur shoes or blue suede shoes. Just mindless consumerism. They'd rather not be free, they'd rather be told what to do, because that's what appeared to us was the case."

However, fate intervened when radio stations in the Southeastern states began playing a track from the album without any push from Devo's record label. Kal Rudman, a Florida-based program director and influential deejay who published a top-40 tip sheet, began promoting "Whip It." The song's title came from an expression the Mothersbaugh brothers frequently heard at home while growing up in Akron.

"Whip It" quickly gained traction on radio playlists. Casale recalled: "It went up the East Coast. Once it hit New York, it was over. Then it went everywhere. We had to stop the tour, recalibrate everything, because suddenly, instead of playing to

House in Akron's Highland Square neighborhood where Devo developed the song, "Whip It."

five hundred or seven hundred people, we were going to play to three to five thousand people."

Consequently, Devo was ordered by Warner Brothers to take a short break in order to shoot a music video for the track. Filmed in Los Angeles over a 16-hour period, the video was inspired by an article in a 1962 issue of *Dude* magazine, which the band had found at a second-hand store in Santa Monica.

Mothersbaugh told the authors of *I Want My MTV*: "'Whip It' was shot in our rehearsal room. The faux log cabin was made out of the cheapest paneling we could find at Home Depot. We cast a band member's girlfriend, and when I was at the mall, I saw a girl who was really pretty and really cross-eyed, so I asked if she'd be in the video. It was casual." The video also featured a flamenco dancer portrayed by 20-year-old Shaylah Spitz-Kalmus, who was paid $200 for her appearance, and an older woman – a Russian immigrant – who held a fruit pie in her hands while uttering the phrase, "Oh, that Alan." Mothersbaugh recalled, "Once we taught her that line... she wouldn't stop saying it."

However, due to the somewhat racy video, MTV viewers found unexpected meanings in the song's lyrics. Mothersbaugh stated at the time: "We find it quite ironic that people were able to misinterpret a Devo song like, allow it to become a hit because of its sadomasochistic overtones. When we wrote the song we didn't even think of it that way." Likewise, Casale explained: "We wrote a lyric that had to do with the self-help, can-do, you're-number-one philosophy of America. It was a parody of the slogan, cliches and limericks that are part of America's folklore tradition. There was no sexual content in that lyric, but people *chose* to interpret the phrase 'whip it' sexually."

The album also featured the track, "Gates Of Steel," a reworked version of "Temple On My Plan," which was co-written by members of a 1960s all-girl rock band from Akron, the Poor Girls. While Mothersbaugh had previously dated a member of the group, Debbie Smith, Casale had dated another member, Sue Schmidt.

Meanwhile, "Whip It" would peak at #14 on *Billboard's* pop chart and was voted the number-one song of the year in 1980 by the listeners of the nation's most influential new wave radio station, KROQ in Los Angeles. With Devo finally achieving a level of respect, *Freedom Of Choice* placed at #43 on *New Musical Express'* ranking of the Best Albums of the year. And while "Whip It" was Devo's only Gold single for sales of one-million copies, *Freedom Of Choice* was the group's only Platinum-certified album.

In May 1980, Devo performed "Snowball" during an appearance on *American Bandstand*. During a short interview, the show's affable host Dick Clark referred to Devo as "a very unusual group." When he asked if Devo came "from Akron, Ohio," Mark Mothersbaugh responded, "Correct, where the rubber meets the road." That same month, Devo launched a successful tour across Japan before heading to Europe for a month of shows.

▶ CHAPTER 22
GETTING SOME SATISFACTION

After the unexpected success of "Whip It," there was an immediate change in the group's stature in the music industry. Now playing for larger and more boisterous crowds, the members of Devo did not engage in the traditional rock and roll lifestyle. Unlike former Kent resident Joe Walsh, who was renowned for traveling with a chainsaw and destroying hotel rooms, the members of Devo took the opposite route. Jerry Casale described the group's behavior while on tour: "We were always the band that instead of showing up and destroying things, we could fix plumbing that wasn't working or a light socket that had burned out. We always left the campsite cleaner than we found it."

Meanwhile, when the second of two planned Devo concerts in Riverside, California, was cancelled at the last minute due to problems with the group's lighting system, the 3,000-strong crowd became violent. A local newspaper called the incident a "riot... with anything that was loose being picked up and thrown at the windows, the building and the staff. The police soon arrived in riot gear. The concert crowd turned their attention to throwing things at the police, who responded with tear gas." Numerous people were injured, including six police officers.

During this period, the members of Devo appeared on *Word Of Mouth*, the debut album by the group's early supporter, Toni Basil. The project also featured three Devo compositions. Another track, "Mickey," became an international smash hit. That same year, Mothersbaugh and Casale provided backup vocals on the Debbie Harry solo track, "Jump Jump." They were credited as Spud Devo and Pud Devo.

*   *   *   *   *   *

While living in Los Angeles, Mark Mothersbaugh became friends with comedian John Belushi, who had earned his fame as a star on *Saturday Night Live*. The two men had something in common – while Mothersbaugh was raised in Akron, Belushi had visited the city many times in the 1960s and '70s to spend time with his uncle and cousins. During the visits, John Belushi and his brother, Jim, enjoyed driving around the Rubber City.

Meanwhile, Mothersbaugh would soon begin a romantic relationship with another original cast member of *Saturday Night Live*, Laraine Newman, who at the time was starring in the Broadway stage play, *The Fifth Of July*. (In addition to Mothersbaugh, Newman would date a number of notable musicians, including Warren Zevon, Andrew Gold and Johnny Winter.) After first getting to know each other in 1982, Mothersbaugh and Newman dated – off and on – for the next three-years.

Newman portrayed the character Donut Rooter on a 1984 VHS compilation of Devo music videos, *We're All Devo*.

Donut Rooter's onscreen father, Rod Rooter, was an obnoxious music executive whose character was based on the band's experiences at Warner Brothers. He was portrayed by Michael W. Schwartz. Additionally, Timothy Leary – the 1960s LSD guru – portrayed a scientist named Dr. Byrthfood. Leary and Mothersbaugh were close friends at the time. The home video would earn Devo their first and only Grammy nomination.

It was through his relationship with Newman that Mothersbaugh became friends with a young, skinny comedian named Paul Reubens. Both Newman and Reubens were members of the Los Angeles comedy troupe, the Groundlings. During this time, Reubens introduced his onstage alter-ego, Pee-wee Herman. Later, when Reubens was writing the script for his debut feature film, *Pee-wee's Big Adventure*, he asked Mothersbaugh to score the music. Busy at the time, Mothersbaugh turned down the request. Instead, Reubens hired songwriter Danny Elfman of Oingo Boingo.

*   *   *   *   *   *

When Devo entered a studio to record their followup to *Freedom Of Choice*, their record label viewed the band in a new light. Instead of being treated as an art band with limited commercial potential, Devo was now considered a profit maker. Mark Mothersbaugh recalled: "Warner Brothers, when they hired us, they already had like Captain Beefheart and Wild Man Fischer and other people who didn't make any money but were cool art-credibility kind of artists. And we always stayed in the black, but we never made them millions of dollars. So once we made them eight figures, then that changed everything for them. Then on our fourth album, it was like the president of Warner Brothers showed up in the studio, kind of startled us because everyone had left us alone in the past."

However, the members of Devo were not interested in repeating their commercial, mainstream success. Mothersbaugh revealed: "The reality was that Jerry Casale and I, as much as we would like to say 'Oh, we could write a pop song any day of the week,' it wasn't how we thought about music. We didn't think about writing pop songs, we thought about what we wanted to talk about. We didn't write love songs, we didn't write party songs. We wrote songs that related to the bigger message of Devo. And so, in a way, 'Whip It' was the beginning of the end for Devo, in the sense that the record companies really pushed us towards trying to create pop music. It just wasn't our nature."

Additionally, there was another problem. Mothersbaugh wasn't happy about how Warner Brothers was openly fleecing Devo: "They were paying us less money for an audio cassette, but there were [newspaper] articles about how much cheaper it was to make an audio cassette than it was to press vinyl. So I went in and had a meeting with [Warner Brothers chief] Mo Ostin, and said, 'You know, Mo, I need to ask you something really important. Why is it that, in our deal, you have it so you're paying us substantially less money for every audio cassette that you sell than for every piece of vinyl, yet you make a bigger profit?' He just smiled and looked at me like I was his dense naive son. And he goes, 'Because that's the way it is'.... At least he was totally up-front about it. He was totally unashamed and that there was no justification except for power."

The sessions for Devo's fourth album began in December 1980 and continued into April. Although the album was considered self-produced, the band received some assistance during the sessions. Notable producer Larry Alexander recalled: "They came into the Power Station. They'd heard of me and they asked me if I wanted to record their album. They played me a demo of this new album that they were gonna do, and I said, 'That sounds finished! What do you want me to do?' ... What's funny is between recording the demos and these sessions they'd bought all new equipment. They had double mini-Moogs built.... We recorded it in New York, and then we mixed it in Los Angeles at the Record Plant."

The album, *New Traditionalists*, was issued on August 26, 1981. Taking a more synch-pop direction, the album was highlighted by the track, "Through Being Cool." The song's music video was the first on MTV to feature break dancing. Another track, "Beautiful World," featured Casale on lead vocals. In the song's video, Mothersbaugh's character Booji Boy stood at the controls of a video mixer that reviewed a series of major news events from the 20th Century.

During this period, Devo dropped their yellow industrial suits and red energy domes for Japanese-inspired short-sleeved shirts, khaki pants and black rubber pompadour wigs. Although the wigs were patterned after John F. Kennedy, most fans misattributed them to the newly elected president, Ronald Reagan. Devo also introduced another of its signature images – the Happy Astronaut – which was borrowed from a vintage, paper Halloween mask.

For their next tour, Devo constructed an elaborate stage set that merged a Roman-style temple with elements of a modern fast-food restaurant. And instead of their usual choreographed robotic moves, the band members performed as they walked on treadmills. Casale explained: "We always thought it was appropriate for Devo to be walking on treadmills. Walking fast and going nowhere. I think it's a nice statement."

At this stage of Devo's career, the group preferred to tour without an opening act. Casale recalled: "We didn't really like opening acts. If we had to, we always tried to get an opening act that was not a typical band. We didn't want somebody onstage making as much noise as we were about to make, burning out the crowd's ears. We had interesting, weird stuff. We even tried comedians and weird acrobatic acts, things that the crowd would boo at. We did have a four-piece chamber group play classical versions of our songs – that was great fun. People liked that."

Meanwhile, Devo nearly reached the U.S. top-40 for a second time when the single, "Working In A Coal Mine," stalled out at #43. The track – a remake of the 1966 top-10 hit by New Orleans R&B singer Lee Dorsey – was featured in the animated film, *Heavy Metal*. Although Warner Brothers chose not to include the track on *New Traditionalists*, the label later relented and included a bonus 45rpm single of the song along with the album.

▶ CHAPTER 23
NEW TRADITIONALISTS

Shortly before the release of *New Traditionalists*, MTV had arrived on cable television. Several months earlier, the members of Devo had been persuaded by the network to allow the *free* use of the group's early videos. Mark Mothersbaugh told the authors of *I Want My MTV*: "By the time MTV showed up, it was something Devo had been anticipating for half a decade. We predicted that there was going to be music television, and when it showed up, we were going to use it to blow away all the Tom Pettys and ZZ Tops and Van Halens. But those bands wound up using video much more efficiently than we ever did." Likewise, Gerald Casale revealed: "From 1974 onwards we didn't even really want to make records; we wanted to make video discs with film shorts.... When they said they were going to do this kind of thing with MTV, we were so elated and thought, 'Now we're going to be able to do what we want. We can make feature films.'"

To compensate Devo for the airing of their videos, MTV featured the band in one of the network's first contests. Viewers were vying for the opportunity to win a five-day holiday in

Hawaii with the members of Devo. This gave the group a great deal of free publicity. However, when veejay Martha Quinn selected the winning postcard, she sported a confused expression on her face after realizing that the winner, Dolli Quattrocchi Gold, was from Akron, Ohio! Determined to win the prize, Gold had mailed postcards on a daily basis.

* * * * * *

Becoming a worldwide sensation, Devo toured across New Zealand and Australia in early-1982. During a stop in Melbourne, the group appeared on the television show, *Countdown*, and lip-synced a pair of songs, "Whip It" and "Workin' In A Coal Mine."

The group's fifth album – *Oh, No! It's Devo* – was released later in 1982. Recorded at Cherokee Studios in Los Angeles, the project was produced by Roy Thomas Baker, who was best known for his work with the Cars, Queen, Journey and Foreigner. At the time, Jerry Casale discussed the group's musical progression: "We're not static, just as the people in our audience are not static.... You can take the boys off the farm but you can't take the farm out of the boys. We have restructured the shape and switched the emphasis but we're still the spuds from the Midwest, pissed off, with a plan."

On the album's cover, the members of Devo introduced a new look – round, white, oversized "spud ring" collars, which were mocked in the press for their resemblance to toilet seats. Additionally, they fully embraced their spudness by substituting potatoes in place of their bodies.

However, the album was met with indifference by radio and

earned just a three-star rating from *Rolling Stone*. Nevertheless, videos of the singles – "That's Good" and "Peek-A-Boo!" (which featured Spazz Attack) – received some airplay on MTV. However, MTV refused to air the original version of the video for "That's Good" due to a sexually provocative scene. As such, Devo reluctantly agreed to edit the video.

Meanwhile, Devo had finally perfected their multimedia stage act, which they debuted at the Universal Amphitheatre in Los Angeles. Casale explained the complexity of the group's stage performances during this time: "We had rear projected sixteen-millimeter film... and we had six tracks of sound dubbing connected to it from a thirty-five-millimeter sound dubber that would come through our monitors with click tracks so we were in sync with the videos playing on the screen behind us. We had characters in the videos singing background vocals and doing things right on cue, matching the climaxes in the music. Mark would turn around and interact with people onscreen and shoot them with a ray gun and they would evaporate. The audiences loved it."

However, at a sold-out performance in Houston on November 30, things did not go well. Casale was called to the side of the stage and warned by police to stop the show or otherwise he'd be arrested. But when the band suddenly launched into another song, Casale and their stage manager were subsequently arrested and spent the night in a freezing jail cell.

In 1983, Devo landed their third and final chart hit on *Billboard's* Hot 100 with "Theme From Doctor Detroit," from the comedy film of the same name starring Dan Aykroyd. That same year, Devo made an appearance on the Sarah Jessica

Parker sitcom, *Square Pegs*. On the episode, the group was hired to perform at a party for Muffy Tepperman (played by Jami Gertz). Devo lip synced "That's Good," but were banned by network censors from airing the song's video in the background.

▶ CHAPTER 24
SO LONG, WARNER BROTHERS

In February 1984, Devo released their sixth album, *Shout*. It was recorded over a ten-month period at the Record Plant in Los Angeles. With improved recording technology, the individual band members were now able to record in the studio by themselves, which inadvertently damaged the cohesion within the group.

The album's front cover featured Timothy Leary's son, Zachary, who was credited as Zachary Chase. The back cover featured Bob Mothersbaugh's daughter, Alex. Once again, Devo introduced new stage uniforms – which were described as Chinese-American Friendship Suits.

Finally, popular music had caught up to Devo as dozens and dozens of electronic synthesizer bands were embraced by both MTV and top-40 radio. But when *Billboard* magazine compared *Shout* to the music of Thomas Dolby, the members of Devo were not amused. Casale remarked: "We've been around long enough for people to take bits and pieces of what we've been doing and make them into commercially palatable things. To the press, we sound like these people because they really sound like us."

The album's first single, "Are U Experienced?," was a remake of the Jimi Hendrix classic. The song's music video, which cost $50,000, featured a professional Hendrix impersonator, Randy Hansen. However, the video featured a controversial scene in which Hansen emerged from a coffin to perform a guitar solo.

At the end of 1984, Devo parted with their management team and entered into a dispute with their label, which wasn't sufficiently promoting the group. Consequently, *Shout* was the group's lowest-charting album up to that point. Casale recalled: "It was like we were just left on a clothes line, hanging out to dry." The Hendrix controversy combined with poor album sales angered the heads of Warner Brothers, which decided to offer Devo a sum of $250,000 to terminate their recording contract. Suddenly, just as new wave was dominating popular music, Devo was left without a record label.

Despite their limited mainstream success, Devo had no intention of altering how they created music. Mothersbaugh recalled: "I remember at the time, reading this article about Sting. And he said, 'you know, I can wake up in the morning and have breakfast and by... lunchtime, I've got a top-10 radio hit written.' And I just remember thinking, 'how do you even think about music like that? How do you think that's what you want to do?' For me it was always a foreign concept to write like that."

Although the members of Devo were ambivalent about scoring pop hits, former Akron resident Marilyn Martin would soon top *Billboard's* Hot 100. She teamed with Phil Collins in 1985 on the hit single, "Separate Lives," which was featured on the soundtrack of the film, *White Nights*. Later working as a backing vocalist, she would tour with both Joe Walsh and Stevie Nicks. Martin also provided the prominent backing vocal on the Tom Petty and Heartbreakers' hit, "Don't Come Around Here No More."

▶ CHAPTER 25
THROUGH BEING COOL

Drummer Alan Myers would leave Devo in 1985. He was unhappy with his diminishing role within the band. The album, *Shout*, had featured far more drum machines than any previous Devo album. Jerry Casale recalled: "I begged him not to quit Devo. He could not tolerate being replaced by the Fairlight [synthesizer and sampler]. Losing him was like losing an arm." The band had spent $35,000 to purchase the then state-of-the-art instrument. As a result of Myers' sudden departure, the group abandoned plans for a tour and a long-form video of the album's songs.

After leaving Devo, Myers subsequently found work as an audio engineer. He later changed fields and became an electrical contractor. Occasionally returning to music, he briefly joined what he described as a "scary cabaret band."

By the mid-1980s, Devo had essentially disbanded. With Mark Mothersbaugh and Jerry Casale writing more than 80-percent of Devo's material, the earnings from the group's publishing rights kept both of them financially afloat. Every time a Devo song aired on radio or television, the two men made money. However, Bob Mothersbaugh wasn't as financially secure. He later formed an unsuccessful band that played Devo songs as well as various rock oldies. Eventually, he joined his brother's successful production company. Bob Casale, meanwhile, turned to independent production work and oversaw projects by Andy Summers of the Police and the punk band, the Vandals. Eventually, Casale would also join Mark Mothersbaugh's firm.

During this period, the group was referenced in one of the most popular films of the decade, *Back To The Future*. When Doc Brown (Christopher Lloyd) emerged from his souped-up DeLorean in the parking lot of the Twin Pines Mall, he was wearing an industrial suit. An amused Marty McFly (Michael J. Fox) asked Brown if he was wearing a Devo outfit.

Back in Akron, Al Mothersbaugh – the cousin of the Mothersbaugh brothers in Devo – had joined a popular local rock band, the Twist-Offs. Much like Devo, the Twist-Offs frequently caused mayhem at their shows. Due to their unpredictable antics – such as telling the audience to bomb the stage with beer bottles – the group was banned from a number of Northeastern Ohio venues.

Unsure if Devo would ever reunite, Mark Mothersbaugh recorded his first solo album, *Music For Insomniacs*, which was released only in Japan. Soon after, he began creating music for television shows and films. After receiving another request to work with actor/comedian Paul Reubens, Mothersbaugh had a change of heart and agreed to provide the music for the Saturday morning children's program, *Pee-wee's Playhouse*.

Initially, Mothersbaugh began working on the show's theme song: "I made the mistake of telling Pee-wee I'd write theme songs until he was absolutely sure he'd gotten the right one. I spent two weeks writing 13 different songs, including heavy metal and rap versions. Then he decided the first one was the best." Casale recalled: "Mark and I went to New York to record the title track with Cyndi Lauper. Her boyfriend/manager tried to talk her out of it, because he only wanted her to do 'serious' stuff at that time. But fortunately, she'd already agreed to do it for Paul, and pulled out her squeaky voice again."

Mothersbaugh also began providing the background music for the weekly series: "Working with Paul Reubens was the best introduction to scoring for a guy who'd never scored anything before. He was very supportive. If something had to be weird, I made it really weird, and if it had to be sad, I'd make it really sad." Mothersbaugh also recalled: *"Pee-wee's Playhouse* was the perfect show because I could do mash ups between classical and polka and metal and punk and opera and bachelor pad music... and it was all acceptable, and it was all fair game." He described his weekly routine: "I'd received the tape of the upcoming episode on Tuesday from New York. We'd record on Wednesday, send it back on Thursday. The score would be cut into the show on Friday and air on Saturday. Compared to the cycle I was used to with Devo – compose 12 songs, rehearse, record, rehearse for the tour, go touring for months, and then start it again – this was great. I thought, 'I love TV!'" Mothersbaugh would provide the background music for all five-seasons of the series.

Years later, Mothersbaugh would lament: "Something like *Pee-wee's Playhouse* couldn't happen again – someone like Paul [Reubens] getting creative control over his show. Now there are so many filters that by the time any program actually airs, so many people have peed on it that it's a big yellow stain."

▶ CHAPTER 26
AN ENIGMA

Eventually, the members of Devo realized they wanted to record another album. Having parted with Warner Brothers, the group was faced with some unexpected challenges. Jerry Casale explained at the time: "We thought we would just come back and get another deal with another record company, but that turned into an adventure. The scene had changed, MTV had a new position in the marketplace, and a new crop of bands had come in. People's tastes were going toward something else, something totally different." The new wave groups of the classic MTV era had been replaced by a series of hair metal bands, which in just a few years would be supplanted by grunge and alternative rock acts.

After a two-year hiatus, Devo reconvened in 1987, with former Sparks drummer David Kendrick brought in to replace Alan Myers. For their first effort, the group recorded the soundtrack of the horror flick, *Slaughterhouse Rock*, which starred Toni Basil. Also that year, Devo released an album of instrumental, elevator music versions of their best-known material, *E-Z Listening Disc*. Previously, the tracks were only available on a pair of cassettes that were offered through Club Devo. Casale explained: "What could be more devoluted than becoming a Muzak band?"

Landing a recording contract with Enigma, Devo fared poorly at their new label. Gravitating toward dance-rock, the group tried to adapt to the changing tastes in popular music. Casale recalled: "We didn't quite know where to go. It gets ugly. It gets weird. Business does you in. I wanted to make huge, primitive, frightening Led Zeppelin-style songs but with the same lyrical content. Some of the other guys [in the band] weren't comfy with it and the record company were saying, 'Give us another 'Whip It!'' We left Warners and Enigma gave us a deal."

Released in May 1988, the album, *Total Devo*, was poorly received. A *Rolling Stone* reviewer wrote: "Much of this attempted comeback album seems to be a desperate SOS from main writer Mark Mothersbaugh." The project featured a surprise remake, Elvis Presley's "Don't Be Cruel." Mothersbaugh defended the decision to record the song: "Elvis was more Devo than we could have ever been."

Devo's relationship with their new label quickly went downhill. The group was also forced to deal with a public image problem. As Casale recalled: "The mythology that the press preferred to present about Devo is that we were incredibly clever, incredibly devious, incredibly deliberate and self-aware and that we were playing a game on the music industry, hoodwinking them, playing a prank on them. Now, of course, that has its inevitable backlash."

Also that year, Devo launched their first tour in five-years. Taking a step backward, the group played mostly clubs and smaller theaters. Mothersbaugh complained at the time: "It really feels like we're starting over.... We're staying in Motel 6s, and we have the smallest crew we've ever had. We would have done a big show, but we just couldn't work out a sponsorship. We have no money. It's not like in the past when we had records on the radio. We're making the best of it.... I think Enigma has our best interest at heart but we're used to having a publicist on the road with us and things being set up along the way, and that's not the case here. It's like the difference between driving a brand-new BMW and a 12-year-old Toyota."

In November, Devo returned to Northeastern Ohio for an appearance at Peabody's Down Under in Cleveland. The show opened with acoustic versions of three of the group's classic songs, including "Jocko Homo." A reviewer lamented the fact that the performance was "lacking the helter skelter edginess that once characterized Devo's unique stage presence."

Unfortunately, Devo's misfortunes continued. The group's 1990 album, *Smooth Noodle Maps*, was a flop and failed to chart on *Billboard*. A single from the album, "Post Post-Modern Man," bombed on the pop charts, but did reach the top-10 on *Billboard's* Modern Rock chart.

Not surprisingly, Devo disbanded for a second time. Mothersbaugh explained: "We had signed a bad record deal with a company that was going bankrupt. And it was just all these things happening at once. We had gone through a number of disappointing things within the band and outside of the band and with the business of the band. We decided we just couldn't take our managers anymore, our lawyers. They didn't understand what we were about."

During this period, the members of Devo – except for Bob Mothersbaugh – appeared in the comedy film, *The Spirit Of '76*. The film spoofed the popular culture fads of the 1970s and featured an all-star cast that included Leif Garrett, David Cassidy and Rob Reiner. The film, which was set in the year 2176, featured Mothersbaugh and Casale as members of the Ministry of Knowledge. After a magnetic storm destroyed all traces of history, a team led by Cassidy attempted to go back in time and witness the country's founding in 1776. Instead, the team accidentally landed in 1976.

▶ CHAPTER 27
MUTATO MUZIKA

Mark Mothersbaugh quickly emerged as a prolific jack-of-all-trades. He launched a very lucrative Los Angeles-based production company in 1989 called Mutato Muzika. The name was taken from the combination of two Devo symbols – mutant and potato.

In the book, *Cartoon Music*, Mothersbaugh explained: "There were other composers that worked with me. At the time I started, I was doing four or five TV shows a week. I was doing a show for Disney, a child's show called *Adventures In Wonderland*. On that show, we needed a number of composers because the schedule of the production was so fast – two new underscores and eight songs per week. I'd say, 'I can't write eight songs a week.' And they said, 'Well, you must have some friends that you would trust to work with you.' So I got the other Devo guys; my brother Bob and Bob Casale both came on board and started working with me on the show. We ended up with twenty composers writing songs, including Bill Mumy, you know, Will Robinson [from *Lost In Space*]. The show was a lot of fun, and it changed my thinking about scoring from being a guy sitting in his bedroom with one keyboard. My studio took over the house. There were two studios in the house, and then I got the house next door and put a studio there."

In 1995, the growing company settled into a large, 9,500-square-foot, circular building – which was constructed in 1969 by its former tenant, a plastic surgeon – on Sunset Strip in West Hollywood, not too far from the legendary Whisky a Go-Go nightclub. Mothersbaugh described the structure, which was designed by notable architect Oscar Niemeyer, as a "cross between a hovering space ship and a miniature version of the LA Forum." A reporter described the facility in more artistic terms: "The Mutato Muzika building in West Hollywood is painted Day-Glo green and looks like a tipped-over hamster wheel, with mirrored windows as rungs that make the building seem like it's constantly spinning. Beneath the main-floor recording studio is a big, cluttered circular room. To enter you pass a threshold guarded by a Speed Racer rug, and beyond this threshold is a sight that would give the Klaxons or Datarock a conniption."

Heading the company, Mothersbaugh was able to harness his vast experience in the fields of film, graphics and music. However, he faced an unexpected aggravation: "Early on with the company, we had clients coming in, expecting me to be wearing the red energy-dome hat. That was the problem of being in a band that stumbled onto a little bit of pop success."

While Devo had spent the last two decades mocking, attacking and spoofing big business, Mothersbaugh was now earning a very good living by creating ad campaigns, shooting commercials and providing music for television and films. *The*

Mark Mothersbaugh at the MOCA gala in Los Angeles.

New York Times reported: "To resolve some of the contradictions between his earlier band and his current line of work, Mr. Mothersbaugh said that for a while he would slip subversive messages into his advertising music. He claimed to have inserted a subliminal voice saying 'sugar will rot your teeth' into a commercial for Gummi Savers. He said he also added 'avoid consumption' to a campaign for BMW and 'biology is destiny' to a cosmetics commercial."

Consequently, Mothersbaugh was now able to spread his message on a grander scale – and get paid handsomely for his efforts. He explained at the time: "It gives us a chance to write music and be involved in pop culture at a more subversive level.... You write music for an ad on Monday, and on Saturday 20 million people are listening to it." Over the next three-decades, he helped to create literally hundreds of television commercials and advertising campaigns for companies such as Apple, Nike, Lexus, McDonald's and Coca-Cola.

Mothersbaugh also worked on dozens of television shows. He was brought into the *Rugrats* franchise when series creator Gabor Csupo asked to use some tracks from Mothersbaugh's solo album, *Music For Insomniacs*. Instead, Mothersbaugh offered to create new music for the program. Soon, Mark and his brother, Bob, were providing music for multiple seasons of the series. They also wrote the program's catchy opening theme song. And in an ironic twist, Mothersbaugh wrote the theme song for the shortlived 1998 television series, *The Mr. Potato Head Show*. Airing on Fox, the program lasted just one season.

Mothersbaugh also provided music for a number of films, including *The Lego Movie, Rushmore, Herbie: Fully Loaded, The Royal Tenenbaums, 21 Jump Street* and several Wes Anderson features.

Mothersbaugh also continued to engage in his lifelong love of art by displaying his work at various galleries around the country. In 1994, before a gallery show in Detroit, he said: "I'm at the point in my life I only do things I like to do. I don't have to do *Saturday Night Live* or go on tour if I don't want to. I like showing my art preferably in a little gallery... where art is really seen, rather than in a big gallery in New York. That is not pleasant for me. There will be kids here tonight, not the entrenched art mafia." At the same time, he admitted: "I have a pretty cool day job. I get to work with very creative people, and it changes all the time, which is fun. And I've worked on a system where I come into work a couple hours early, and I have two hours all to myself to write music just for me or work on visual art just for me. And then everybody shows up at 9 and we go to work and score whatever it is we're working on today. And it's kind of nice to have a day job that supports being an artist that I don't have to be running out and trying to figure out how to make money off my art."

While Jerry Casale was constantly seeking to reunite Devo, Mothersbaugh enjoyed stepping back from his role as a stage performer. He told a reporter: "No matter how obsessed you are, the music business can destroy your spirit. When we last toured Europe, someone put *Spinal Tap* on the tour video bus, and I started counting the number of similarities between us and them.... I felt it was time to move on."

▶ CHAPTER 28
A REUNION

After a five-year break, Devo briefly reformed in 1995 to record the track, "R U Ready," for the film, *The Mighty Morphin Power Rangers*, as well as a new version of "Girl U Want" for the film, *Tank Girl*. The following year, Devo returned to the stage for occasional short tours and one-off performances, beginning with an appearance at the Sundance Film Festival. Needing a drummer, the group hired Josh Freese.

However, with the members of Devo now in their 40s, Mothersbaugh was concerned about the reactions of audiences: "We didn't know what to expect. But people seemed to like us. The crowds were disappointingly well behaved. We were hoping they'd be lightning rods of hostility like in the old days." After the first stop on the short tour, Mothersbaugh retired his Booji Boy character for the next several years.

Also in 1996, Devo performed at Lollapalooza – minus their traditional, synchronized robotic dance moves. Opening with "Whip It" and closing with "Gates Of Steel," the group had gained a new legion of fans. Mothersbaugh stated at the time: "We wear the same yellow outfits we wore in 1977 when we

Jerry Casale at the unveiling of a large portrait of Devo by Janet Macoska in downtown Akron.

first came out. We do the same show and we actually sound better than we did then. We always wore those yellow outfits that made us look like cheeseburgers. Now, a couple of us look like double cheeseburgers mixed in with the single cheeseburgers."

During the Lollapalooza tour in 1997, Devo performed at Blossom Music Center in Cuyahoga Falls – a suburb of Akron. Mothersbaugh recalled at the time, "My brother Bob and I used to ride the bus from our parents' house in Northampton Township past the Blossom property every morning on our way to school. I remember going to some of the first concerts there in '68."

Jim Ellis, the editor of *Cle* magazine, wrote in *Cleveland Free Times*: "It's kind of funny. I was watching a special on Lollapalooza and the kids were going nuts over Devo. They were up there looking well fed and a little middle-aged but still doing all the same moves, just like twenty years ago. Only now the kids are twenty years younger than they are." Also on the Lollapalooza bill were Korn, James, Snoop Dogg, Tricky and a band with Akron connections, Tool, which was headed by Maynard James Keenan of nearby Ravenna. (In appreciation of the Akron Spud Boys, Keenan named his son, Devo.)

Despite the positive feedback from audiences, Mothersbaugh was troubled by something that occurred when Devo was onstage: "All the other acts came out and watched us. And then, as we were playing, I realized they were looking at me in the same way I looked at Chuck Berry when I met him in college. Like we were relics from a different era."

A few years later, Casale openly complained that Mothersbaugh was the reason why Devo wouldn't reform on a permanent basis: "He can score a film and make tons of money, but he doesn't want to put his butt on the line where you're up against the capricious whims of rock critics, unscrupulous promoters and all the vermin who screwed us and ripped us off in the record business. I don't blame him in that sense."

* * * * * *

In the new millennium, musical acts were forced to license their songs to advertisers in order to survive. Mark Mothersbaugh defended the practice of placing Devo songs in television commercials: "My feeling about that stuff is that it's a way to plant little tiny brain bombs, that will go off later in people's heads, in people's minds – people that would never listen to Devo, people that were like 'Oh, Devo is some bullshit art band.'"

However, when McDonald's introduced a Happy Meal character named New Wave Nigel – wearing a miniature red energy dome on his head – the members of Devo were not amused. The cap had been designed and trademarked by Casale years earlier. Consequently, Devo threatened to sue the restaurant chain for trademark infringement

Meanwhile, the members of Devo decided to record an album under an alias – the Wipeouters. Mothersbaugh recalled: "[I wrote] a theme song for a TV series called *Rocket Power* that was about skateboards and surfboards. I thought, 'Wait a minute. We were in a band in junior high, before Devo, that did all surf music.' The other guys that were in the Wipeouters originally all work here, so after hours we set up our gear and we played those songs again. So what started off as a theme song turned into a whole album."

In the mid-1960s, the Wipeouters were forced to disband after Mothersbaugh's father decided to store the family's Christmas tree in the spot where the band's drum set had stood. Mothersbaugh recalled, "He sabotaged our ability to rehearse."

▶ CHAPTER 29
THE NEW DEVO

In 2006, Disney introduced Devo 2.0 – a school-age version of the band aimed at pre-teens. More than 1,000 children auditioned to join what Jerry Casale described as the "next generation spud." Dressed in modified Devo costumes, the five youths recorded a 12-track CD and accompanying DVD, which were released by Walt Disney Records. Casale recalled that the lyrics of the group's classic songs were cleaned up by Disney: "We're in a post 9/11 world now, so irony isn't allowed. When you work for the mouse, you do what the mouse tells you to do. We never got to meet their censorship board. There was no discussion. We couldn't ask why.... It's like a Rorschach blot where it tells you more about their minds than ours."

That same year, Devo reconvened to record a cover version of the Nine Inch Nails hit, "Head Like A Hole," for the soundtrack of the Jackie Chan film, *Supercop*. But just like many of Devo's previous efforts, the project was poorly promoted.

Also that year, Casale released a solo album, *Mine Is Not A Holy War*. For the project, he adopted the stage name, Jihad

Jerry & The Evildoers. The album featured seven original songs as well as updated versions of four lesser-known Devo songs. Also included was a remake of the Yardbirds classic, "He's Always There." However, Casale explained the negative reaction to the project: "The album was met with a lot of fear from people who didn't get what I was doing. I was doing a show on Sirius radio and the deejay told me if it was a Devo album, he could play some of the cuts, but not as Jihad Jerry."

Meanwhile, Mark Mothersbaugh suddenly decided he wanted to be a father: "I adopted two kids.... The moment I saw these kids, a door opened in my brain that I didn't even know was there. It took me over 50 years to understand what it was about that made people want to load this planet with more people. I totally understand it now, it's hardwired into you. It's a reptilian thing to be a parent." He traveled to China with his wife, Anita Greenspan, to adopt a pair of young girls.

*   *   *   *   *   *

In 2007, Devo enjoyed an unexpected revival after recording the single, "Watch Us Work It," which was used in a commercial for Dell Computers. It was their first single in seventeen-years. Mark Mothersbaugh recalled: "Everyone heard that song and said, 'Is that Devo?' and we started getting a lot of calls." Consequently, the band went back on the road.

In May 2008, Mothersbaugh returned to Kent State University to receive an honorary degree. When he dropped out in 1973, he was just one-quarter short of earning a Bachelor's degree. (In 2001, the school also gave an honorary degree to Joe Walsh, who dropped out when he was a junior.)

Anita Greenspan and Mark Mothersbaugh at the Art of Elysium Heaven Gala in Los Angeles.

Later in 2008, a reunited Devo belatedly returned to Akron for a political fundraising concert that was staged at the city's architectural jewel – the 3,000 seat Akron Civic Theater, which had opened in 1929 as a Loew's theater. Also performing that

Devo at the Akron Civic Theater in 2008.

night were the Black Keys and Chrissie Hynde. This would mark the only time Akron's three most famous rock acts would appear on the same bill. As for why Devo took so long to perform in their hometown, Casale admitted: "They never got us. We didn't play there in 30 years because no one would come."

After a few remarks by a pair of local politicians, Devo – the headliner – took the stage. A reporter for *LA Weekly* observed: "The big Loew's movie screen drops and one of Devo's great propaganda films appears. The crowd cheers as clips of the band throughout its many incarnations flip on the screen. Images of the band in the early days, marching through

The Akron Civic Theater.

abandoned Akron warehouses, of cruising through ragtag streets in junky Chevys, of jerking back and forth to music. The screen rises and Devo, heavier than in the film but still donning the requisite yellow-and-red getups, tear into 'That's Good,' a song with an honest simplicity that either candidate would be smart to steal.... Many of these songs, Mothersbaugh tells the crowd, were written five blocks from the Civic Theatre."

Amid much publicity, Devo released their ninth album in June 2010, *Something For Everybody*. The project took nearly two-years to record. Wanting to satirize the business of entertainment, the group used traditional marketing strategies and employed focus groups while working on the album.

Casale explained: "With music being devalued in the culture, people feeling they shouldn't even have to pay for it, and record companies not doing their job to bring the best music forward, it just seemed like the only art left for Devo was to embrace all these corporate business techniques." Peaking at number-30 on *Billboard's* sales chart, the album was not a strong seller. Mothersbaugh explained: "At the same time, 500 albums came out the week our album came out. How does somebody get noticed in all that?"

Devo enjoyed some high-profile gigs in 2010, beginning, with a performance at the opening ceremonies of the Winter Olympics in Vancouver, Canada. It was the group's first television appearance in two-decades. Mothersbaugh meekly announced at the time: "We think now might be Devo's time, or so we're hoping." Devo also appeared at the Coachella Music and Art Festival before kicking off a tour with a stop at the Lollapalooza Festival in Chicago.

Mothersbaugh said at the time: "Touring is one of those things where, when you're in your 20s, it's great, and I think every 20-year-old should be in a band with a #1 hit once in their life, and get to go out on stage in front of a hundred thousand people. It's kind of exciting! When you're in your 30s, it's kind-of old. When you're in your 40s, you shouldn't be doing it anymore."

▶ CHAPTER 30
BEAUTIFUL WORLD

In 2013, Devo re-released a limited-edition album, *Hardcore*, which compiled the group's unreleased early material, mostly from 1974 to 1977. Due to the unexpected fan interest, the band decided to perform the songs in concert. Casale revealed at the time: "[We] talked about this as an idea because we were both amazed at the number of sales which we were generating off the release of these basement tapes really. Between the vinyl and the CD, it was something like 50,000 copies that got sold, and these days, nothing really sells, so we thought: 'Wow, there's really interest in the roots of Devo. Nobody's ever seen us play them' ... Being insulated (in Ohio) we just did anything we could think of. And the stuff is all over the map; it's politically incorrect, it's funny."

Devo suffered a pair of tragedies during this period. Former drummer Alan Myers died in June 2013. And the following February, guitarist Bob Casale (Bob 2) died suddenly from heart failure.

In 2014, Devo launched a 10-date North American tour. Although initially conceived as a 40th anniversary tour, the

Booji Boy swarm at the DEVOtional convention in Akron.

renamed Hardcore Devo tour featured songs from the group's early period. Casale stated at the time: "We've been going back and reexamining who in the heck we were in a more innocent time when no one cared who Devo was. I think it's going to be a little bit unhinged and raw but that is how we started. This wouldn't appeal to the crowd that just wants the same Devo show. In fact some may not like it and some might start screaming, 'Whip It, Whip It,' but that's not going to happen. We were the White Stripes and Black Keys when those guys were in diapers." However, the group encountered a problem.

Casale revealed: "It's kind of difficult, because we would have needed Bob to play a lot of those [early] songs properly. So we picked songs that we could pull off as a foursome." One of the performances, which was staged at the Fox Theatre in Oakland, California, was issued on DVD.

Josh Hager joined the band in August 2014. He had previously appeared on the group's album, *Something For Everybody*. At his debut appearance at the United Center in Chicago, Hager was initially slated to work as an off-stage backing musician – on guitar and keyboards. But just a few minutes before showtime, he was asked by Mothersbaugh to take the stage with the rest of Devo. Hager was given the stage name, Josh 2, while drummer Josh Freese was dubbed Josh 1. Meanwhile, Robert Mothersbaugh Sr. – better known by Devotees as General Boy – passed away in May 2016 at the age of 90. His wife, Mary, had passed away two-years earlier.

In July 2018, Devo came out of retirement to play at a festival in San Francisco, Burger Boogaloo, which was emceed by the notoriously outlandish filmmaker, John Waters. Mothersbaugh stated at the time: "This is a one-off thing, absolutely. As far as doing something beyond that? We'll see what happens. I love creating music and creating art more than performing the same show over and over again, which is kind of what happened with Devo.... I'd be OK if we didn't do this again." For the performance, Fred Arminsen joined on drums.

Unlike Jerry Casale, Mothersbaugh was not fond of taking the band back on the road. Worse yet, Mothersbaugh hinted at the time that this would be the band's final concert. Eventually, Devo would sporadically return to the stage, usually at large music festivals.

CHAPTER 31
HALL OF SPUD

In 2018, Devo was belatedly nominated for induction into the Rock and Roll Hall of Fame for the first time. However, they were not inducted. After the group earned a second nomination in 2021, April 1 was named "Devo Day" by the mayor of Akron. Over the next month, red, oversized Devo-style energy domes constructed of stacked tires were placed all over the Rubber City in an attempt to encourage the Hall of Fame's voters to induct the band. But again, the group was snubbed.

When the pandemic hit in 2020, Devo was forced to cancel several scheduled shows, including an appearance in Cleveland. In June of that year, Mark Mothersbaugh barely survived a bout of Covid. He spent eighteen-days in an ICU ward, during which time he experienced a series of hallucinations. *The Los Angeles Times* reported: "While attached to the ventilator, he said: 'I wrote a whole new Devo album and put together a whole live show.' In his hallucination, the band performed it on the streets of Hollywood – through the use of augmented reality. 'We were standing on top of these projections, which were growing

The Rock and Roll Hall of Fame in Cleveland.

somehow.'"

Although Mothersbaugh beat the virus, he suffered an unexplained permanent injury: "Somewhere along the line I got hit in the eye, so now my right eye is just a souvenir. It doesn't really function as an eye anymore. That's kind of unfortunate."

Devo played just three shows in the Covid year of 2021. Mothersbaugh said at the time: "I don't miss playing live shows. I feel like we toured so many years and traveled so many years that we kind of did what we were supposed to do, and I just think it's kind of odd for Devo to be playing shows this late, but we're gonna do some."

Meanwhile, the Rock and Roll Hall of Fame again nominated Devo. In April 2022, after the group's third nomination, Jerry Casale stated: "It feels good to be recognized even by some self-appointed official body.... But on the other hand, if we don't get in I wouldn't be surprised. We're used to that. It would be nice to get in now instead of getting in posthumously."

Likewise, Mothersbaugh said: "It's nice to be acknowledged for the things you've done. We know what we did, but it's nice when other people know what you did, too." When asked how he would celebrate if the group was inducted, Mothersbaugh cryptically responded: "There's a parking lot right next door [to the museum] – I will go and ask if I can buy one parking space and own it. Ohio has really lax burial laws – this is the truth. In Ohio, you can basically bury your grandma in your backyard and grandpa in the front yard if you want. I'll keep that space open for anybody who ever played in Devo. They can all get buried in that one space next to the Rock and Roll Hall of Fame."

Yet again, Devo didn't make the final cut. Instead, two other new wave acts were inducted – the Eurythmics and Duran Duran – both of which had formed long after Devo.

*   *   *   *   *   *

In retrospect, 74-year-old Jerry Casale proclaimed in 2022: "We were an alternative act before there was a name for alternative acts. Our popularity was based on word of mouth, coming to our live shows, people buying our records, and people playing our records for their friends who also had to have the record. 'Whip It' was the only thing to break through into the mainstream world where you had to have a top 40 hit." Additionally, he declared: "Devo was an art collective, so the songs we wrote were coming from a place of innovation and discovery. It wasn't like sitting down going, 'We got to write a hit, that sounds like what's happening on the radio.' We didn't do that. So we stood the test of time, and a lot of our songs are more relevant now than they were 40 years ago. They mean more to people because De-evolution turned out to be real."

Meanwhile, in April 2023, Devo celebrated the 50th anniversary of their first performance. Sadly, there was little recognition of the event in either Akron or Kent. That year, Devo launched what was billed as their Farewell Tour.

*   *   *   *   *   *

As for the theory of de-evolution – which the members of Devo had predicted in the 1970s – Mark Mothersbaugh stated: "It's unfortunate that our philosophies were proven true. I would have wished that we could have been proven wrong. We didn't enjoy the idea that things were devolving. We thought that we were just musical reporters telling everyone that the boat is leaking and that there are problems in our DNA that need to be fixed. Unfortunately, we've watched the world not adjust to it."

▶ EPILOGUE

In addition to Devo, a number of other notable Akron rock acts – such as Chrissie Hynde and the Black Keys – were innovative rebels who went against the grain of popular music. While Hynde combined the punk aesthetic with strong melodies and the Black Keys turned their backs on mainstream radio with their combination of blues and low-fi alternative rock, Devo had a far more rebellious goal – to transform society with their doctrine of de-evolution.

Jerry Casale proclaimed: "Devo were fearlessly original. We were what was 'new' about new wave. We defined ourselves, and we stayed on-message at a time when that was frowned upon in rock and roll. We were also DIY – we created custom merchandise, we put out manifestos – and we were laughed at and highly criticized." Likewise, Mark Mothersbaugh insisted: "I think we were atypical. We weren't really New Wave and we weren't really punk and we weren't really rock and roll or dance music per se. We had a different kind of energy and our band was created out of trying to find a way to describe what we saw going on in the world."

However, the group paid a very high price for refusing to

bend to commercial demands and instead choosing to embrace music as a traditional art form. As a result, Devo managed to score just one top-40 hit during their lengthy career, when "Whip It" landed on pop charts in 1980. Casale lamented: "Other than good critical acceptance and our fan base, radio shut us out. Mainstream rock press hated us. But everything we did is now stock and trade for a generation of bands. People look back now and listen to us more openly." Ironically, countless MTV-era, new wave acts that were directly influenced by Devo would have far greater success on radio playlists. And yet Devo were not the recipients of accolades, awards or even respect for their innovative melding of modern art, electronic music, film, costumes and choreography.

Despite leaving Akron in the late-1970s, the members of the group remained attached to the Rust Belt city. In 2016, when the mayor of Akron presented Devo a key to the city, Mothersbaugh told the assembled crowd: "Whether I'm in

London working on a film or in South America playing with a band, people think of us as Akronites.... I hope you guys don't mind me representing you."

▶ BIBLIOGRAPHY

1. Devo. (1993). *The Complete Truth About De-evolution* (DVD). Rhino.
2. Faris, Mark. (1984, January 15). Rubber City talent shines in spotlight. *The Akron Beacon Journal*.
3. "Gerald V. Casale: Devo Provocateur." (2023, March). *Mojo*.
4. Gray, Chris. (2011, March 23). Devo in jail: Bassist Gerald Casale talks 1982 U of H arrest. *HoustonPress*.
5. Huhn, Mary. (2001, April 28). Are we not men? We are Wipeouters. *The New York Post*.
6. Madonio, Chas. (2022). *Bars, Bands, and Rock 'n Roll: The Golden Era in Kent, Ohio*. Kent, OH: Kent Historical Society Press.
7. Musarra, Russ. (2000, February). The Akron centeseptequinary celebration. *Northern Ohio Live*.
8. Nagy, Evie. (2015). *33 1/3: Devo, Freedom of Choice*. New York: Bloomsbury Academic.
9. Peters, Matt. (2005, Spring). Devo: The truth about Devo's de-evolution. *The Burr*.
10. Popoff, Martin. (2015, February 20). Devo bassist celebrates release of 'Miracle Witness Hour.' *Goldmine*.
11. Price, Mark J. (2004, September 20). Clark Gable got his act together in Rubber City before he hit road to Hollywood. *The Akron Beacon Journal*.
12. Prufer, Jason. (2019). *Small Town, Big Music: The Outsized Influence of Kent, Ohio, on the History of Rock and Roll*. Kent, OH: Kent State University Press.
13. Reynolds Howard, Victoria. (2000, March). Mothers of Invention. *Northern Ohio Live*.
14. Roland, Mark. (2018, August). Devo: 'Q: Are We Not Men? A: We Are Devo." *Electronic Sound*.
15. Schulps, Dave. (2023, February 12). Gerald V. Casale: Devo's invisible man returns. *Trouser Press* [online].
16. Sheppard, David. (2008). *On Some Faraway Beach: The Life and Times of Brian Eno*. Chicago: Chicago Press Review.
17. Talevski, Nick. (2009). *Hang on Sloopy: The History of Rock and Roll in Ohio*. Green, OH: Guardian Express Media.
18. Talevski, Nick; & West, Robert. (2010). *The Origins and Early History of Rock & Roll*. Green, OH: Guardian Express Media.
19. Thomas, Nick. (2021). *Joe Walsh: From the James Gang to the Eagles*. Guardian Express Media: Green, OH.
20. Warwick, Neil; Kutner Jon; & Brown Tony. (2004). *The Complete Book of the British Charts, 3rd ed.* London: Omnibus Press.
21. Whitburn, Joel. (2008). *Rock Tracks 1981-2008*. Menomonee Falls, WI: Record Research.
22. Whitburn, Joel. (2018). *Top Pop Albums 1955-2016*. Menomonee Falls, WI: Record Research.
23. Whitburn, Joel. (2019). *Top Pop Singles 1955-2018*. Menomonee Falls, WI: Record Research.

▶ NOTES

INTRODUCTION
1. "where you fall down on..." ~ Harvey, Allan. (c. 1990). *Night After Night* (The Comedy Channel).
2. "So they came. By foot..." ~ Junod, Tom, (1992, December). Oh, what a night! *Life*.
3. "Virtually overnight, this super-salesman..." ~ Irwin, Theodore. (1957, July). Rock 'n' roll'n Alan Freed. *Pageant*.
4. "It's in the center of..." ~ Savage, Jon. (1978, March 4). Devo: Are we not ready? *Sounds*.

CHAPTER 1: MARK MOTHERSBAUGH
1. "Of all the bands who..." ~ Long, Pat. (2009, May 1). We are legend. *The Guardian*.
2. "Devo was a self-contained concept..." ~ Shore, Michael. (1984). *The* Rolling Stone *Book of Rock Video*. New York: Quill.
3. "Perhaps they are the antithesis..." ~ McClintock, Tom. (1977, December 15). Devo: New and outrageous. *The Camden Courier-Post*.
4. "Devo is not ahead of..." ~ Michaels, Sean. (2010, February 23). Devo plan comeback album through focus group. *The Guardian*.
5. "The teacher would say: 'Read..." ~ Fussman, Cal. (2014, February). Mark Mothersbaugh. *Esquire*.
6. "I couldn't read the big..." ~ Rogers, John. (2000, September 11). Kid stuff lures new wave of Devo-tees. *The Portland Press Herald*.
7. "I could remember five minutes..." ~ Litt, Steven. (2016, May 13). Q&A with Devo's Mark Mothersbaugh, whose 'Myopia' show opens soon at two NEO museums. *The Cleveland Plain Dealer*.
8. "The next day when I..." ~ Kane, Dan. (2016, May 26). Devo's Mark Mothersbaugh is focus of major art retrospective. *The Canton Repository*.
9. "I thought music was something..." ~ "Devo-ted to little Rugrats: Mark Mothersbaugh used to front a popular new wave band; now he makes music for kids." (2000, November 15). *Waterloo (Ontario, Canada) Region Record*.
10. "I was sitting at the..." ~ Unsworth, Renee. (2012, September 20). Mark Mothersbaugh interview. *The St. Augustine Record*.
11. "We were awful, of course." ~ Rogers, John. (2000, September 11). Kid stuff lures new wave of Devo-tees. *The Portland Press Herald*.
12. "A guy from Cuyahoga Falls..." ~ Hynde, Chrissie. (2015). *Reckless: My Life as a Pretender*. New York: Doubleday.
13. "They were so strict at..." ~ Reynolds Howard, Victoria. (2000, March). Mothers of Invention. *Northern Ohio Live*.
14. "I really disliked all my..." ~ Peters, Matt. (2005, Spring). Devo: The truth about Devo's de-evolution. *The Burr*.
15. "I went back there recently..." ~ Bierman, William. (1975, February 2). Artist making his stamp by updating past's images. *The Akron Beacon Journal*.
16. "I used to go to..." ~ Vaziri, Aidin. (2018, June 25). Pop quiz: Devo on reuniting for Burger Boogaloo and how its weird songs became modern classics. *The San Francisco Chronicle*.

CHAPTER 2: JERRY CASALE
1. "The '60s come along and..." ~ Abram, Malcolm X. (2018, February 15). Devo co-founder reflects on dad's death. *The Akron Beacon Journal*.
2. "I saw every act when..." ~ Blade, Richard. (2021). *The Lock Down Interviews*. Los Angeles: Bladerocker Books.
3. "My parents had no use..." ~ Greene, Andy. (2020, May 4). Devo's Jerry Casale looks back at Kent

State 50 years later: 'Time stood still.' *Rolling Stone*.
4. "There was this small clique..." ~ Greene, Andy. (2020, May 4). Devo's Jerry Casale looks back at Kent State 50 years later: 'Time stood still.' *Rolling Stone*.
5. "The political movement on campus..." ~ Greene, Andy. (2020, May 4). Devo's Jerry Casale looks back at Kent State 50 years later: 'Time stood still.' *Rolling Stone*.
6. "I was drafted in 1967..." ~ Greene, Andy. (2020, May 4). Devo's Jerry Casale looks back at Kent State 50 years later: 'Time stood still.' *Rolling Stone*.
7. "Art is intended to make..." ~ (2010, October 1). Devo cofounder stresses the importance of keeping artistic relevance. *Daily Kent Stater*.
8. "It was a very creative..." ~ "Joe gains honorary Doctorate." (2002, January). *Natural Progressions*.
9. "'Are you the guy who..." ~ Kane, Dan. (2016, May 26). Devo's Mark Mothersbaugh is focus of major art retrospective. *The Canton Repository*.
10. "We started talking about what..." ~ Niesel, Jeff. (2016, May 18). Rubber City rebel: Inside Mark Mothersbaugh's magical world of mutants, monsters and mongoloids. *Scene*.
11. "We had really similar aesthetics..." ~ Peters, Matt. (2005, Spring). Devo: The truth about Devo's de-evolution. *The Burr*.
12. "We clicked from the very..." ~ Reynolds Howard, Victoria. (2000, March). Mothers of invention. *Northern Ohio Live*.
13. "For [Casale's] senior art project..." ~ Popson, Tom. (1982, December 12). Devo: Four spuds with alternative information. *The (McAllen, TX). Monitor*.

CHAPTER 3: KENT STATE
1. "We took these big garbage..." ~ Kahn, Ashley; George-Warren, Holly; & Dahl, Shawn (Eds.). (1998). *Rolling Stone: The Seventies*. New York: Little, Brown and Company.
2. "One irate motorist gunned his..." ~ "At war with war." (1970, May 18). *Time*.
3. "Without bothering to consult Kent..." ~ "At war with war." (1970, May 18). *Time*.
4. "Anyone who lived in Kent..." ~ Hynde, Chrissie. (2015). *Reckless: My Life as a Pretender*. New York: Doubleday.
5. "It was the first warm..." ~ Mervis, Scott. (2020, May 8). Four dead in Ohio. *The Toledo Blade*.
6. "It seemed that the campus..." ~ "At war with war." (1970, May 18). *Time*.
7. "We had no idea there... ~ "10 questions for... Devo's Gerald Casale." (2006, December 8). *Goldmine*.
8. "everybody stopped dead in their..." ~ Crowe, Cameron. (1975, February 27). Joe Walsh, child of the silent majority: Ex-James Gangster tends to his garden. *Rolling Stone*.
9. "I don't think (the shooting)..." ~ Zonkel, Phillip. (2000, February 9). A chat with Chrissie Hynde: Protestor to Pretender. *The Los Angeles Daily News*.
10. "It was a fork in..." ~ Mervis, Scott. (2020, May 8). Four dead in Ohio. *The Toledo Blade*.
11. "May 4 derailed a lot..." ~ Sommer, Tim. (2018, May 4). How the Kent State massacre changed music. *The Washington Post*.
12. "Everything was falling apart. Everything..." ~ Mueller, Andrew. (2010, August). Devo: You say you want a de-evolution. *Uncut*.
13. "Having been there for..." ~ Ross, Curtis. (2010, July 16). Devo's co-founder now excited by future. *The Tampa Tribune*.
14. "That's when Devo was born..." ~ Lester, Paul. (2015, January). Devo. *Prog*.
15. "We were intrigued by this..." ~ Koehler, Robert. (2014, January 15). Mark Mothersbaugh: Devolution becomes him. *Variety*.
16. "So it is that the..." ~ Lewis, Bob. (1972, n.d.). Readers vs. breeders: Didactical works re De-Evolution. *LA Staff*.

CHAPTER 4: DEVO'S DEBUT
1. "I started playing the blues..." ~ Reynolds, Simon. (2010). *Totally Wired: Post-Punk Interviews and Overviews*. New York: Soft Skull Press.
2. "It was like something out..." ~ Van Matre, Lynn. (1978, October 29). Gimmicks, rough rock, and Booji Boy: And that's Devo. *The Chicago Tribune*.
3. "I told him I wasn't..." ~ Lester, Paul. (2015, January). Devo. *Prog*.
4. "We were looking for a..." ~ Fussman, Cal. (2014, February). What I've learned: Mark Mothersbaugh. *Esquire*.
5. "We thought, 'If we called..." ~ Reynolds, Simon. (2010). *Totally Wired: Post-Punk Interviews and Overviews*. New York: Soft Skull Press.

CHAPTER 5: PHILOSOPHY OF DEVO
1. "[Jim] created a homemade electronic..." ~ Reynolds, Simon. (2006). *Rip It Up and Start Again*. New York: Penguin Books.
2. "Devo makes a triumphant return..." ~ "Devo clan returns triumphant." (1974, April 23). *Daily Kent Stater*.
3. "the infantile spirit of devolution" ~ Roberts, Randall. (2007, December 5). Are you not Devo? You are Mutato. *LA Weekly*.
4. "Mark and I had started..." ~ Willman, Chris. (2010, August). The secret history of Devo. *Spin*.
5. However, the poster's bawdy design... ~ Zimmerman, Sue. (1970, January 20). Poster controversy burns. *Daily Kent Stater*.
6. "He had written 'Sloppy,' and ..." ~ Reynolds, Simon. (2005). *Rip it Up and Start Again: Postpunk 1978-1984*. New York: Penguin.

CHAPTER 6: THE EARLY YEARS
1. "We were not musicians. We..." ~ Jancik, Wayne. (1998). *The* Billboard *Book of One-Hit Wonders* (rev. ed.). New York. Billboard Books.
2. "When we first started together..." ~ "Devo: For the fighters as they attempted to conquer the problems." (1978, no. 7). *Search & Destroy*.
3. "We got into experimenting with..." ~ Davis, Michael. Are they not keyboardists? Mark Mothersbaugh and Bob Casale. (2008). [In *Keyboard Presents: The Best of the '80s*, Rideout, Ernie; Fortner, Stephen; & Gallant, Michael (Eds.)] New York: Backbeat Books.
4. "Devo, from the beginning, was..." ~ Freeman, Paul. (2011, August 25). *The (Palo Alto, CA) Daily News*.
5. "Bob Mothersbaugh... doesn't say much..." ~ Mueller, Andrew. (2010, August). Devo: You say you want a de-evolution. *Uncut*.
6. "It wasn't until '75 when..." ~ Reynolds, Simon. (2010). *Totally Wired: Post-Punk Interviews and Overviews*. New York: Soft Skull Press.
7. "We were real excited, we..." ~ "Devo: For the fighters as they attempted to conquer the problems." (1978, no. 7). *Search & Destroy*.
8. "Mark and Jerry drove out..." ~ Nagy, Evie. (2015). 33 1/3: *Devo, Freedom of Choice*. New York: Bloomsbury Academic.
9. "When we played him a..." ~ Martin, Richard. (1999, May). Is he not Mark Mothersbaugh? *CMJ New Music Monthly*.
10. "I was at the bar..." ~ Heaton, Michael. (2003, November 14). 'Are We Not Men' captures allure that drew Devotees. *The Cleveland Plain Dealer*.
11. "The school lore is that..." ~ Reynolds Howard, Victoria. (2000, March). Mothers of Invention. *Northern Ohio Live*.
12. "We were called crazy, cynical..." ~ Mueller, Andrew. (2010, August). Devo: You say you want a de-evolution. *Uncut*.

13. "He's never heard us..." ~ Fricke, David. (1978, December 5). D-E-V-O are not P-U-N-K. *Circus*.
14. "They hated us from the..." ~ Bahadur, Raj. (1981, October 29). Duty now for the future. *Scene*.

CHAPTER 7: DEVO, THE FILM MAKERS

1. "In 1974, Jerry Casale, his..." ~ Marks, Craig; & Tannenbaum, Rob. (2011). *I Want My MTV*. New York: Dutton.
2. "We ran into these suits..." ~ Popson, Tom. (1982, December 12). Devo: Four spuds with alternative information. *The (McAllen, TX) Monitor*.
3. "What we saw as being..." ~ Mervis. Scott. (1999, February 5). The re-evolution or Devo. *The Pittsburgh Post-Gazette*.
4. "They don't breathe at all..." ~ Todd, Ryan. (2006, Winter). Interview with Gerald Casale of Devo. *KDViationS*.
5. "They had the concept for..." ~ Shore, Michael. (1984). *The* Rolling Stone *Book of Rock Video*. New York: Quill.
6. "He wasn't trying to be..." ~ Abram, Malcolm X. (2014, February 19). Bob Casale 1952-2014: Keyboardist, guitarist for Devo remembered. *The Akron Beacon Journal*.

CHAPTER 8: AT THE CRYPT

1. "There were two places we..." ~ Willman, Chris. (2010, August). The secret history of Devo. *Spin*.
2. "They have about 30 people..." ~ Pantsios, Anastasia. (1977, May 6). Punk rockers. *The Cleveland Plain Dealer*.

CHAPTER 9: JOCKO HOMO

1. "I remember looking at them..." ~ Roberts, Randall. (2018, July 12). The art of de-evolution: Mark Mothersbaugh and Gerald Casale discuss two new books that celebrate punk band Devo's visual work. *The Los Angeles Times*.
2. "It was always our performance..." ~ Pinnock, Tom. (2015, March). The making of... Jocko Homo. *Uncut*.
3. "Mark wrote 'Jocko Homo' pretty..." ~ Pinnock, Tom. (2015, March). The making of... Jocko Homo. *Uncut*.
4. "I was driving around Ohio..." ~ McCormick, Carlo. (2000, n.d.). Devolved dynamo of the American soundscape: Mark Mothersbaugh. *Seconds Magazine*.
5. "an afternoon of music, discussion..." ~ "Weekend calendar." (March 12, 1977). *The Akron Beacon Journal*.

CHAPTER 10: PUNK OR NEW WAVE?

1. "Punk rock was fashioned in..." ~ Jenkins, Mark. (1989, June 28). Gems from the Rust Belt. *The Washington Post*.
2. "We were punk in the..." ~ Sommer, Tim. (2018, May 4). How the Kent State massacre changed music. *The Washington Post*.
3. "The only way we fit..." ~ Sanders, Tony. (2009, no. 64). Devo: The Devo chronicles, Part Two!: Historians of the future. *The Big Takeover*.
4. "Pere Ubu didn't like us..." ~ Sanders, Tony. (2009, no. 64). Devo: The Devo chronicles, Part Two!: Historians of the future. *The Big Takeover*.
5. "In 1975, *Creem* magazine would..." ~ Colegrave, Stephen; & Sullivan, Chris. (2005). *Punk: The Definitive Record of a Revolution*. London: Cassell Illustrated.
6. "The word 'punk' goes back..." ~ Colegrave, Stephen; & Sullivan, Chris. (2005). *Punk: The Definitive Record of a Revolution*. London: Cassell Illustrated.
7. "I said why don't we..." ~ Colegrave, Stephen; & Sullivan, Chris. (2005). *Punk: The Definitive Record of a Revolution*. London: Cassell Illustrated.

8. "I like the Ramones; don't..." ~ Popoff, Martin. (2022, August/September). Love from a lonely boy. *Goldmine*.
9. "Bands didn't want to be..." ~ O'Brien, Glenn. (1986, January). Debbie's back. *Spin*.
10. "We needed all the help..." ~ Stein, Seymour. (2018). *Siren Songs*. New York: St. Martin's Press.

CHAPTER 11: IN NEW YORK CITY
1. "was the perfect atmosphere for..." ~ Roland, Mark. (2018, August). Devo: 'Q: Are We Not Men? A: We Are Devo. *Electronic Sound*.
2. "By that point, because we..." ~ Schwachter, Jeff. (2005, August 11). Catching up with Devo. *Atlantic City Weekly*.
3. "I remember early on in..." ~ Roland, Mark. (2018, August). Devo: 'Q: Are We Not Men? A: We Are Devo. *Electronic Sound*.
4. "[We] got into a fight..." ~ Savage, Jon. (1978, March 4). People in general – Devo in particular: Are we not ready? *Sounds*.
5. "They were playing to audiences..." ~ Mueller, Andrew. (2010, August). Devo: You say you want a de-evolution. *Uncut*.
6. "[Lennon] was with Ian Hunter..." ~ Roland, Mark. (2018, August). Devo: 'Q: Are We Not Men? A: We Are Devo. *Electronic Sound*.
7. "Somebody from a record company..." ~ Ellefson, David. (1997). *Making Music Your Business: A Guide for Young Musicians*. San Francisco: Miller Freeman.
8. "There was really not enough..." ~ Hagelberg, Kymberli. (1991, April 4). Punk rock, the pink triangle and the birth of the Akron sound. *Scene*.
9. "Devo are another batch of..." ~ Pantsios, Anastasia. (1977, May 6). Punk rockers. *The Cleveland Plain Dealer*.
10. "We got pretty lousy feedback..." ~ Winbush, Don. (1977, July 17). 'Punk rock' is music the all-American way. *The Akron Beacon Journal*.

CHAPTER 12: IN LOS ANGELES
1. "We came out here and..." ~ Lewis, Pat; & Kidd, Tom. (1988, August 6). DEVOted to subversion: The true story of the pioneers who got scalped by the system. *Music Connection*.
2. "This was at a time when..." ~ Robins, Wayne. (1978, October 29). Rocking out of Akron. *Newsday*.
3. "Every record company started coming..." ~ Roland, Mark. (2018, August). Devo: 'Q: Are We Not Men? A: We Are Devo. *Electronic Sound*.
4. Although stories widely vary as... ~ Adams, Deanna R. (2002). *Rock 'n' Roll and the Cleveland Connection*. Kent, OH: Kent State University Press.
5. "What we really wanted to..." ~ Norman, Michael. (1997, July 18). Devotion: Local boys who made good headliner at Lollapalooza. *The Cleveland Plain Dealer*.
6. "He wanted to record our..." ~ Garden, Joe. (1997, July). Mark Mothersbaugh. *The Onion*.
7. "I was a huge fan of..." ~ Carlisle, Belinda. (2011). *Lips Unsealed*. New York: Crown.
8. "We'd seen the picture postcards..." ~ "The Billboard.com Q&A: Devo." (2007, January 18). *Billboard*.

CHAPTER 13: DAVID BOWIE & BRIAN ENO
1. "Then afterwards, he said, 'Yeah...'" ~ Collins, Dan. (2009, November 4). Devo: Gonna be a man from the moon. *L.A. Record*.
2. "What I saw in them..." ~ Mieses, Stanley. (1978, May 20). Eno, before and after. *Melody Maker*.
3. "Seven months ago one of..." ~ Scott, Jane. (1977, December 2). Devo: Out of spud fire. *The Cleveland Plain Dealer*.
4. "We saw it all go..." ~ Ruskin, Zack. (2018, June 28). What the world needs now is Devo. *SF Weekly*.

CHAPTER 14: SPUDBOYS VS. THE MUSIC INDUSTRY
1. "Branson called me up in..." ~ Spitz, Marc; & Mullen, Brendan. (2001). *We Got the Neutron Bomb: The Untold Story of L.A. Punk*. New York: Three Rivers Press.
2. "I couldn't stop laughing and..." ~ Simpson, Dave. (2022, April 14). Devo: 'Richard Branson almost killed us in the Jamaican mountains.' *The Guardian*.
3. "I've thought about it since..." ~ Matheson, Whitney. (2009, March 23). Q&A: Devo answers your questions! *USA Today*.
4. "If that had happened, Devo..." ~ Dalton, Stephen. (2010. June 12). Devo, the devoted prankster, reunite. *The Times of London*.
5. "In retrospect, I wish we..." ~ Skye Fadroski, Kelli. (2022, April 26). Devo asks, Are we not meant to be in the Rock and Roll Hall of Fame? *The Pasadena Star-News*.

CHAPTER 15: IN GERMANY
1. In exchange for producing the... ~ Devo, (2003). *The Complete Truth About De-Evolution* (DVD). Rhino Entertainment.
2. "It was outside of Cologne..." ~ Weiss, Pete. (2010, November/December). Devo in the Studio: Gerald and Bob Casale w/ Hager Bros. *Tape Op*.
3. "David kept up with everything..." ~ Jones, Dylan. (2017). *David Bowie: A Life*. New York: Crown Archetype.
4. "He wanted it to be..." ~ Blueskye, Brian. (2019, August 22). Desert Daze may be your last chance to see Devo. 'No plans' for farewell tour, bassist says. *The Palm Springs Desert Sun*.
5. "They were a terrifying group..." ~ Gill, Andy. (1998, June). To infinity and beyond. *Mojo*.
6. "In '77, we had five..." ~ Mervis. Scott. (1999, February 5). The re-evolution or Devo. *The Pittsburgh Post-Gazette*.
7. "The punk bands decided we..." ~ Lester, Paul. (2016, January 21). Devo, White Town, Babybird: What happens when your cult pop band gets huge? *The Guardian*.
8. "We made a mistake by..." ~ Roland, Mark. (2018, August). Devo: 'Q: Are We Not Men? A: We Are Devo. *Electronic Sound*.
9. "We'd only played small clubs..." ~ Simpson, Dave. (2022, April 14). Devo: 'Richard Branson almost killed us in the Jamaican mountains.' *The Guardian*.

CHAPTER 16: ARE WE NOT MEN?
1. "suddenly stood up and started..." ~ Padgett, Ray. (2017, September 25). The story behind Devo's iconic cover of the Rolling Stones' 'Satisfaction.' *The New Yorker*.
2. "People thought it was a..." ~ Blade, Richard. (2021). *The Lock Down Interviews*. Los Angeles: Bladerocker Books.
3. "One guy goes, 'Here's the...'" ~ Conner, Thomas. (2010, August 2). Whip smart; Devo's brainy rockers try to reinvent the music-biz. *The Chicago Sun-Times*.
4. "a brittle, small masterpiece of..." ~ Carson, Tom. (1978, November 30). Evolving with Devo: Are we not amused? *Rolling Stone*.
5. "It was a wonderful gulp..." ~ Lester, Paul. (2015, January). Devo. *Prog*.
6. "We're all Devo. Devo is..." ~ Considine, J.D. (1978, October 24). Devo: The sound of things falling apart. *The Baltimore Sun*.

CHAPTER 17: LEAVING AKRON
1. "It's like a scientific experiment..." ~ Cromelin, Richard. (1979, July 1). Spud report: Devo does its duty. *The Los Angeles Times*.
2. "They played to a sell-out..." ~ Schruers, Fred. (1978, November 5). *Rolling Stone* notes. *The Poughkeepsie Journal*.

3. "If you liked Devo, it..." ~ Crisafulli, Chuck. (1997, June 6). Were they not men? They were Devo. *The Kenosha News*.
4. "There were throngs of people..." ~ Lester, Paul. (2015, January). Devo. *Prog*.
5. "Of course, we came to..." ~ Donofrio, Steve. (2019, October 7). Devo's Gerald Casale talks his favorite new artists, Desert Daze and Axl Rose. *OC Weekly*.
6. "Devo was voted the Worst..." ~ Scott, Jane. (1979, February 9). Springsteen sweeps WMMS/Plain Dealer poll. *The Cleveland Plain Dealer*.

CHAPTER 18: THE AKRON SOUND

1. "Employment in Akron rubber companies..." ~ Musarra, Russ. (2000, February). The Akron centeseptequinary celebration. *Northern Ohio Live*.
2. "One of my clearest memories..." ~ Warner, Brad. (2007). *Sit Down and Shut Up*. Novato, CA: New World Library.
3. "If you went high up..." ~ James, LeBron; & Bissinger, Buzz. (2009). *Shooting Stars*. New York: Penguin.
4. "It's kind of a strange..." ~ Uitti, Jacob. (2022, May 11). The Black Keys: Brothers in arms. American Songwriter.
5. "I think it was all..." ~ Guarino, Mark. (2006, October). Blues brothers. *Harp*.
6. "[Schrader] was having me take..." ~ Hagelberg, Kymberli. (1991, April 4). Punk rock, the pink triangle and the birth of the Akron sound. *Scene*.
7. "When I visited Ohio in..." ~ Christgau, Robert. (1978, April 17). A real new wave rolls out of Akron. *The Village Voice*.
8. "A lot of people came..." ~ Hagelberg, Kymberli. (1991, April 4). Punk rock, the pink triangle and the birth of the Akron sound. *Scene*.
9. "The exposure was a great..." ~ Faris, Mark. (1991, August 11). When the world heard Akron singing. *The Akron Beacon Journal*.
10. "I liked Patty Donahue's deadpan..." ~ Majewski, Lori; & Bernstein, Jonathan. (2014). *Mad World: An Oral History of New Wave Artists and Songs That Defined the 1980s*. New York: Abrams Image.
11. "Tin Huey had done very..." ~ Majewski, Lori; & Bernstein, Jonathan. (2014). *Mad World: An Oral History of New Wave Artists and Songs That Defined the 1980s*. New York: Abrams Image.
12. "It was so great when..." ~ Holdship, Bill. (2003, September). Basic instinct. *Mojo*.
13. "We were arrogant enough to..." ~ Andersen, Sunny M.; & Chanel, Kevin. (1999, no. 3). In conversation with Poison Ivy & Lux Interior. *Girlyhead*.
14. "A lot of other hardcore..." ~ Warner. Brad. (2007). *Sit Down and Shut Up: Punk Rock Commentaries on Buddha, God, Truth, Sex, Death & Dogen's Treasury of the Right Dharma Eye*. Novato, CA: *New World Library*.
15. "You can tell the difference..." ~ Faris, Mark. (1980, March 23). The Akron Sound. *The Akron Beacon Journal*.
16. "I doubt if the locals..." ~ Niesel, Jeff. (2004, October 6). Akron city limits: The Black Keys have brought glory back to the Rubber City. *The Cleveland Free Times*.

CHAPTER 19: DEVO & NEIL YOUNG

1. "It was sort of [a]..." ~ Young, Neil. (2012). *Waging Heavy Peace: A Hippie Dream*. New York: Blue Rider Press.
2. "He's really a strange and..." ~ Reynolds, Simon. (2006). *Rip It Up and Start Again*. New York: Penguin Books.
3. "we met Dennis Hopper and..." ~ Sanders, Tony. (2009, no. 64). Devo: The Devo chronicles, Part Two!: Historians of the future. *The Big Takeover*.

4. "There's a scene where I'm..." ~ Mueller, Andrew. (2010, August). Devo: You say you want a de-evolution. *Uncut*.
5. "That was just such an..." ~ Donofrio, Steve. (2019, October 7). Devo's Gerald Casale talks his favorite new artists, Desert Daze and Axl Rose. *OC Weekly*.

CHAPTER 20: DUTY NOW FOR THE FUTURE

1. "I [had] started to use..." ~ Scott, Ken; & Owsinski, Bobby. (2012). *Abbey Road to Ziggy Stardust*. Los Angeles: Alfred Music Publishing.
2. "Most of the concepts on..." ~ Marsh, Dave. (1979, September 20). Devo destroyed: *Duty Now For The Future*. *Rolling Stone*.
3. "I think, if anything, that..." ~ Hill, Michael. (1980, October). Booji can't fail: They're still Devo – are you? *New York Rocker*.
4. "We were critical darlings with..." ~ Beviglia, Jim. (2018). *Playing Back the 80s*. Lanham, MD: Rowman & Littlefield.
5. "just under 200,000 in the..." ~ Horowitz, Amy. (1979, September). Devo: Are we not businessmen? *Trouser Press*.
6. "The hats came from a..." ~ Conner, Thomas. (2000, April 30). 'Pioneers' of the new pop. *Tulsa World*.
7. "turning into a punk version..." ~ Morse, Steve. (1981, November 5). Devo challenges the treadmill. *The Boston Globe*.

CHAPTER 21: FREEDOM OF CHOICE

1. "We were starting to explore..." ~ Beviglia, Jim. (2018). *Playing Back the 80s*. Lanham, MD: Rowman & Littlefield.
2. "I was sitting in the..." ~ Buskin, Richard. (2013). *Classic Tracks*. London: Sample Magic.
3. "You have to understand that..." ~ Buskin, Richard. (2013). *Classic Tracks*. London: Sample Magic.
4. "if they ever teach a..." ~ Christgau, Robert. (1981, February 2). Christgau's consumer guide. *The Village Voice*.
5. "As it turns out, Devo..." ~ Robins, Wayne. (1980, July 25). Is it Devo? It's a bore. *Newsday*.
6. "We loved that song very..." ~ Wiser, Carl. (2003 December 16). Devo and 'Whip It.' *Songfacts*.
7. "It went up the East..." ~ Beviglia, Jim. (2018). *Playing Back the 80s*. Lanham, MD: Rowman & Littlefield.
8. "'Whip It' was shot in..." ~ Marks, Craig; & Tannenbaum, Rob. (2012). *I Want My MTV: The Uncensored Story of the Music Video Revolution*. New York: Plume.
9. "Once we taught her that..." ~ Kenny, Glenn. (1993, October 14). Whip It: Devo, 1980. *Rolling Stone*.
10. "We find it quite ironic..." ~ Strauss, Duncan. (1981, December 3). 'Nobody wanted us.' *The Sacramento Bee*.
11. "We wrote a lyric that..." ~ McKenna, Kristine. (1982, February). Devo. *Musician*.

CHAPTER 22: GETTING SOME SATISFACTION

1. "We were always the band..." ~ Ryan, Patrick. (2014, June 18). On the road again: Devo carries on amid loss. *USA Today*.
2. "riot was erupting, with anything..." ~ Jarrell Johnson, Kim. (2014, November 1). Back in the day: Riot marred 1980 Devo show in Riverside. *The (Riverside, CA) Press-Enterprise*.
3. "Warner Brothers, when they hired..." ~ Caro, Mark. (2009, November 12). Devo's whipping it in a big way. *The Chicago Tribune*.
4. "The reality was that Jerry..." ~ Ewalt David M. (2014, March 6). Mark Mothersbaugh on making music for TV, games and film. *Forbes*.
5. "They were paying us less..." ~ Garden, Joe. (1997, July). Mark Mothersbaugh. *The Onion*.

6. "They came into the Power..." ~ Crane, Larry. (2013, May/June). Larry Alexander: Diana Ross, Devo, Springsteen, Steely Dan. *Tape Op*.
7. "We always thought it was..." ~ Morse, Steve. (1981, November 5). Devo challenges the treadmill. The Boston Globe.
8. "We didn't really like opening..." ~ Lake, Dave. (2012, April 17). Tell me about that album: Devo's Live in Seattle 1981. *Seattle Weekly*.

CHAPTER 23: NEW TRADITIONALISTS
1. "fit in a little bit with..." ~ Price, Mark J. (2021, May 14). Informal sessions in late-2019 after completing an album for Louisiana singer-songwriter Robert Finley. *The Akron Beacon Journal*.
2. "By the time MTV showed..." ~ Marks, Craig; & Tannenbaum, Rob. (2012). *I Want My MTV: The Uncensored Story of the Music Video Revolution*. New York: Plume.
3. "From 1974 onwards we didn't..." ~ Reynolds, Simon. (2010). *Totally Wired: Post-punk Interviews and Overviews*. New York: Soft Skull Press.
4. "We predicted that there was..." ~ Chonin, Neva. (1998, September 27). Musical Devotion: Twenty years after 'Q: Are We Not Men?,' Devo still making waves. *The San Francisco Chronicle*.
5. "We're not static, just as..." ~ McKenna, Kristine. (1982, February). Devo. *Musician*.
6. "We had rear projected sixteen-millimeter..." ~ Blade, Richard. (2021). *The Lock Down Interviews*. Los Angeles: Bladerocker Books.

CHAPTER 24: SO LONG, WARNER BROTHERS
1. "We've been around long enough..." ~ Alfonso, Barry. (1985, June). The Spud Boys want respect. *BAM*.
2. "It was like we were..." ~ Lewis, Pat; & Kidd, Tom. (1988, August 6). DEVOted to subversion: The true story of the pioneers who got scalped by the system. *Music Connection*.
3. "I remember at the time..." ~ Nagy, Evie. (2015). 33 1/3: *Devo, Freedom of Choice*. New York: Bloomsbury Academic.

CHAPTER 25: THROUGH BEING COOL
1. "I begged him not to..." ~ Perrone, Pierre. (2013, July 6). Alan Myers: Drummer with art-rockers Devo. *The (London) Independent*.
2. "scary cabaret band" ~ Aston, Martin. (1995, October). Devo: Where are they now? *Q*.
3. "I made the mistake of..." ~ Bolles, Don; & Jones, Kim. (1987, July 16). Go, spud, go! *LA Weekly*.
4. "Mark and I went to..." ~ Takiff, Jonathan. (1998, February 27). Devo gives its career some fine-tooning. *The Philadelphia Daily News*.
5. "Working with Paul Reubens was..." ~ "Devo-ted to little Rugrats: Mark Mothersbaugh used to front a popular new wave band; now he makes music for kids." (2000, November 15). *Waterloo (Ontario, Canada) Region Record*.
6. "*Pee-wee's Playhouse* was the perfect..." ~ Ewalt David M. (2014, March 6). Mark Mothersbaugh on making music for TV, games and film. *Forbes*.
7. "I'd received the tape of..." ~ Koehler, Robert. (2014, January 15). Mark Mothersbaugh: Devolution becomes him. *Variety*.
8. "Something like Pee-wee's Playhouse couldn't..." ~ Kelly, Maura. (2005, September). Mark Mothersbaugh. *The Believer*.

CHAPTER 26: AN ENIGMA
1. "We thought we would just..." ~ Lewis, Pat; & Kidd, Tom. (1988, August 6). DEVOted to subversion: The true story of the pioneers who got scalped by the system. *Music Connection*.
2. "What could be more devoluted..." ~ Jancik, Wayne. (1998). *The* Billboard *Book of One-Hit Wonders* (rev. ed.). New York. Billboard Books.

3. "We didn't quite know where..." ~ Stubbs, David. (2000, August). Devo's Jerry Casale. *Uncut*.
4. "Much of this attempted comeback..." ~ Azerrad, Michael. (1988, August 11). Total Devo: Devo. *Rolling Stone*.
5. "Elvis was more Devo than..." ~ Rosen, Craig. (1988, December 7). Devo evolves into new live form. *The Los Angeles Daily News*.
6. "The mythology that the press..." ~ Velazquez, Joe. (1988, October). In the beginning was the end. *Spin*.
7. "It really feels like we're..." ~ Darling, Cary. (1988, December 6). New wave's evolutionaries carry message to the clubs. *The Orange County Register*.
8. "lacking the helter skelter edginess..." ~ Gomez, Brian. (1988, November 17). Devo: Peabody's Down Under, Nov. 8. *Scene*.
9. "We had signed a bad..." ~ Schwachter, Jeff. (2005, August 11). Catching up with Devo. *Atlantic City Weekly*.

CHAPTER 27: MUTATO MUZIKA

1. "There were other composers that..." ~ Goldmark, Daniel. (2002). An interview with Mark Mothersbaugh, in *The Cartoon Music Book* by Goldmark, Daniel; & Taylor, Yuval (Eds.). Chicago: A Capella Books.
2. "cross between a hovering space..." ~ Martin, Richard. (1999, May). Is he not Mark Mothersbaugh? *CMJ New Music Monthly*.
3. "The Mutato Muzika building in..." ~ Roberts, Randall. (2007, December 5). Are you not Devo? You are Mutato. *LA Weekly*.
4. "Early on with the company..." ~ Aquilante, Dan. (1999, June 8). Musically, Mothersbaugh is still kidding around; Rugrats' tunesmith. *The New York Post*.
5. "To resolve some of the..." ~ Strauss, Neil. (2001, April 18). The pop life: Make a myth, whip it good. *The New York Times*.
6. "It gives us a chance..." ~ Crisafulli, Chuck. (1997, June 6). Were they not men? They were Devo. *The Kenosha News*.
7. "I'm at the point in..." ~ Miro, Marsha. (1994, December 11). Member of Devo mines pop culture. *The Detroit Free Press*.
8. "I have a pretty cool..." ~ Thomas, George M. (2023, February 20). Akron native Mark Mothersbaugh lends '80s sensibilities to 'Cocaine Bear' soundtrack. *The Akron Beacon Journal*.
9. "No matter how obsessed you..." ~ Aston, Martin. (1995, October). Devo: Where are they now? *Q*.

CHAPTER 28: A REUNION

1. "We didn't know what to..." ~ Johnson, Kevin C. (1997, July 17). Devo comes home to Akron: Techno band awakens from suspended animation to find that 'De-evolution' is alive and well on Earth. *The Akron Beacon Journal*.
2. "We wear the same yellow..." ~ Mervis. Scott. (1999, February 5). The re-evolution or Devo. *The Pittsburgh Post-Gazette*.
3. "My brother Bob and I..." ~ Norman, Michael. (1997, July 18). Devotion: Local boys who made good headliner at Lollapalooza. *The Cleveland Plain Dealer*.
4. "It's kind of funny. I..." ~ Deluca, Dave. (1997, July 16). Devo-lution. *The Cleveland Free Times*.
5. "All the other acts came..." ~ Walker, Kevin. (1999, November 16). The spirit of Devo lives on and on. *The Tampa Tribune*.
6. "He can score a film and..." ~ Gladstone, Neil. (2000, August). ?&A: Devo's Jerry Casale. *CMJ New Music Monthly*.
7. "My feeling about that stuff..." ~ Schlansky, Evan. (2010, September-October). Devo. *American Songwriter*.

8. "[I wrote] a theme song..." ~ Vaziri, Aidin. (2001, April 22). Pop quiz: Q & A with Devo's Mark Mothersbaugh. *The San Francisco Chronicle.*
9. "He sabotaged our ability to..." ~ Huhn, Mary. (2001, April 28). Are we not men? We are Wipeouters. *The New York Post.*

CHAPTER 29: THE NEW DEVO
1. "We're in a post 9/11 world..." ~ Soeder, John. (2006, March 11). Devo + Disney = kids' new wave. *The Cleveland Plain Dealer.*
2. "The album was met with..." ~ Salkin, Judith. (2011, July 29). Devo whips up a new generation of fans. *The Desert Sun.*
3. "I adopted two kids.... The..." ~ Mulkerin, Andy. (2010, July 8). A conversation with Mark Mothersbaugh of Devo. *Pittsburgh City Paper.*
4. "Everyone heard that song and..." ~ Everett-Green. Robert. (2009, November 23). Does the world need more Devo? *The Globe and Mail.*
5. "De-evolution happened! It's all around..." ~ Leigh, Danny. (2007, June 15). 'We're the house band on the Titanic.' *The Guardian.*
6. "They never got us. We..." ~ Corcoran, Michael. (2009, March 19). An uncontrollable urge to return to stage. *The Austin American-Statesman.*
7. "The big Loew's movie screen..." ~ Roberts, Randall. (2008, October 22). Whip the vote: Devo plays for Obama back home in swingin' Ohio. *LA Weekly.*
8. "With music being devalued in..." ~ Dalton, Stephen. (2010, June 12). Devo, the devoted prankster, reunite. *The Times of London.*
9. "At the same time, 500..." ~ Riemenschneider, Chris. (2010, September 2). Devo's evolution. *The Vancouver Province.*
10. "We think now might be..." ~ Riemenschneider, Chris. (2010, September 2). Devo's evolution. *The Vancouver Province.*
11. "Touring is one of those..." ~ Day, Holly. (2006, no. 58). Devo's Mark Mothersbaugh. *The Big Takeover.*

CHAPTER 30: BEAUTIFUL WORLD
1. "[We] talked about this as..." ~ Larsen, Peter. (2014, June 28). Devo lives up to its name and goes back to the start. *The Orange County Register.*
2. "We've been going back and..." ~ Koshkin, Brett. (2014, June 19). Devo's Jerry Casale looks to the past for the future. *The Village Voice.*
3. "It's kind of difficult, because..." ~ Basedow, Neph. (2014 July 1). Devo Q&A: Gerald Casale. *The Austin Chronicle.*
4. "This is a one-off thing..." ~ Ruskin, Zack. (2018, June 28). What the world needs now is Devo. *SF Weekly.*

CHAPTER 31: HALL OF SPUDS
1. "While attached to the ventilator..." ~ Roberts, Randall. (2020, August 31). Mark Mothersbaugh nearly died from COVID 19. FaceTiming with his family kept him alive. *The Los Angeles Times.*
2. "Somewhere along the line I..." ~ Niemietz, Brian. (2022, May 9). Devo: Making risque 'Whip It' video in 2022 'would be a problem.' *The New York Daily News.*
3. "I don't miss playing live..." ~ Baltin, Steve. (2022, April 3). Sunday conversation: Devo on the Rock Hall nomination, Ukraine, de-evolution coming true 40 years later. *Forbes.*
4. "It feels good to be..." ~ Skye Fadroski, Kelli. (2022, April 26). Devo asks, Are we not meant to be in the Rock and Roll Hall of Fame? *The Pasadena Star-News.*
5. "It's nice to be acknowledged..." ~ Skye Fadroski, Kelli. (2022, April 26). Devo asks, Are we not meant to be in the Rock and Roll Hall of Fame? *The Pasadena Star-News.*

6. "There's a parking lot right..." ~ Callwood, Brett. (2022, April 21). Devo-lution – art-punk pioneers are hopeful on Hall of Fame possibilities. *LA Weekly*.
7. "We were an alternative act..." ~ Blueskye, Brian. (2019, August 22). Desert Daze may be your last chance to see Devo. 'No plans' for farewell tour, bassist says. *The Palm Springs Desert Sun*.
8. "Devo was an art collective..." ~ Baltin, Steve. (2022, April 3). Sunday conversation: Devo on the Rock Hall nomination, Ukraine, de-evolution coming true 40 years later. *Forbes*.
9. "It's unfortunate that our philosophies..." ~ Niesel, Jeff. (2010, June 2). De-evolutionary theory. *Scene*.

EPILOGUE
1. "Devo were fearlessly original. We..." ~ Basedow, Neph. (2014 July 1). Devo Q&A: Gerald Casale. *The Austin Chronicle*.
2. "I think we were atypical..." ~ Stevenson, Jane. (2009 November 24). Devo whips it once again. *The Sudbury (Ontario, Canada) Star*.
3. "Other than good critical acceptance..." ~ Johnson, Kevin C. (1997, July 17). Devo comes home to Akron: Techno band awakens from suspended animation to find that 'De-evolution' is alive and well on Earth. *The Akron Beacon Journal*.
4. "Whether I'm in London working..." ~ Olson, Melissa. (2016, Summer). Evolution of an artist. *Kent State Magazine*.

▶ INDEX

A

Acropolis, 1
The Action, 67, 109, 111
Adventures In Wonderland, 151
Aerosmith, 42
Jane Aire & The Belvederes, 49, 85, 109
Akron, 1-10, 19, 41, 47, 48-50, 51-53, 55, 57, 67, 73, 77, 79, 86, 89, 97, 99-112, 130, 140, 144, 163-164, 171, 174, 176-177
Akron Art Institute, 57
The Akron Beacon Journal, 41, 67
Akron Civic Theater, 91-92, 97, 163-165
The Akron Compilation, 107
Akron Indians, 4
Akron Pros, 4
The Akron Sound, 99-112
Alcoholics Anonymous, 3
Alexander, Larry, 133
A&M Records, 68, 69, 71
American Bandstand, 8, 128
Amin, Idi, 118
Anderson, Wes, 154
Ann Arbor Film Festival, 57
Anthony Wayne Hotel, 101
Arminsen, Fred, 169
Ashley, Jane, 49
Athens, Greece, 1
Athens, Ohio, 23
Auerbach, Dan, 9, 100-101
Aykroyd, Dan, 137
Aylward, Michael, 70
Aylward, Susan, 70
Aztecs, 120

B

Bacharach, Burt, 82
Back To The Future, 144
Bad Company, 43
Baker, Roy Thomas, 136
The Bangles, 107
Bangs, Lester, 60
The Bank, 101-103, 112
Barberton, Ohio, 57
Barger, Ed, 56, 121
Basil, Toni, 70-71, 107, 118, 130, 148
Bators, Stiv, 53
Bawlz, Soo, 118
The Bay City Rollers, 61
The Beatles, 14-15, 19, 67, 118
The Bee Gees, 42
Beefheart, Captain, 17, 20, 59, 131
The Beginning Was The End, 33
Behemoth, Crocus, 57
Bent, Rod, 52
The B-52's, 108
Belushi, Jim, 130
Belushi, John, 130
Berke, Clem, 66
Berlin, Germany, 75
Berry, Ken, 81
Big Apple nightclub, 72-73
Billboard, 14, 128, 137, 139, 140, 149, 166
The Bizzaros, 52, 67, 103, 105
The Black Keys, 9, 101, 108, 164, 168, 175
Blackwell, Chris, 79
Black, Bill, 19
Blank Records, 105
Bleeker Bob's Records, 85

193

Blondie, 61, 63, 66, 67, 70, 82
Blossom Music Center, 158
Blue, David, 95
BMW, 149, 153
Booji Boy, 35-36, 37, 42, 50, 92, 93, 115, 133, 157
Bottom Line nightclub, 96
Bowie, David, 20, 70, 75-76, 79, 83, 117-118
Bowling Balls From Hell, Vols. 1 & 2, 107
Brandt, Elmer, 52
Brown, Doc, 144
Brown, John, 3
Branson, Richard, 80-82, 86-87
Buchtel College, 4
Burger Boogaloo, 169
Burke, Clem, 70
Burroughs, William, 65-66
Butler, Chris, 30, 104, 107, 109
Buzz, Clic, 52
Dr. Byrthfood, 131

C

Cabaniss, George, 108
Canton, Ohio, 35
Capitol Records, 108
Carlisle, Belinda, 72
Carmen, Eric, 15
Carney, Patrick, 108
Carney, Ralph, 101, 108
Carpenter, Bill, 51
The Cars, 91, 97, 136
Cartoon Music, 151
Casale, Robert (Bob), 19, 31-32, 45, 48, 57, 60, 81, 144, 151, 167
Casale, Jerry, 10, 14, 19-22, 25-28, 29-32, 33, 36-37, 39-41, 42, 43, 45-46, 47, 60, 65-66, 67-68, 69, 70, 72, 75, 80, 82, 83, 85, 89, 90-91, 92, 93, 95, 96, 97, 113-115, 118, 120-121, 123-124, 127, 129, 132, 134, 135, 137, 139-140, 143-145, 147-148, 150, 155, 159, 160, 161-162, 166, 167, 169, 172-174, 175, 176-177
Cassidy, David, 150
CBGB, 65-66, 110
Chan, Jackie, 161
Chateau Recorders, 117
Cherokee Studios, 136
Chicago, 8, 62, 166
Chinaman, 37, 118
Chi-Pig, 35, 67, 97, 103, 107, 111
The Choir, 15
Christgau, Robert, 104-105, 124
Jordan Christopher & The Wild Ones, 8
Chrome, Cheetah, 54
The Church of the SubGenius, 35
Cincinnati, 55
Civil War, 3
Clark, Dick, 128
Cleveland, 1, 5-7, 20, 31, 33, 41, 51-53, 57, 59, 70, 72, 97, 102, 149, 171
Cleveland Agora, 70, 96
Cleveland Free Times, 159
The Cleveland Plain Dealer, 67, 76, 97
Cleveland Screaming, 111
Cleveland Stadium, 15
Clone Records, 103, 107
Club Devo, 120, 148
Coachella Festival, 166
Coca-Cola, 154
Cohen, Kip, 68, 69

Cohen, Leonard, 95
Collins, Phil, 140
Columbo (TV show), 61
Columbus, Ohio, 23
Conny Plank Studio, 76
Contents Dislodged During Shipment, 108
The Contortions, 59
Cooper, Alice, 27, 61
Costello, Elvis, 91
Countdown (TV show), 136
Coupe de Ville, 30
Covid, 172
Coxe, Simeon, 17
The Cramps, 68, 110, 111
Creative Arts Festival, 30, 35
Creem magazine, 60-61
Crock, Ray, 3
The Crypt, 51-54, 101, 103, 112
Csupo, Gabor, 154
Cuyahoga Falls, OH, 12, 15, 72
Cuyahoga Falls High School, 29
Cuyahoga River, 53

D

Damage, Donnie, 108, 111
Danceteria, 109
Datarock, 152
Dayton, Ohio, 4
The Dead Boys, 52-54, 60, 62, 66, 108
Dell Computers, 162
Destroy All Monsters, 57
Detroit, 59, 154
Devo Farewell Tour, 174
Devo 2.0, 161
Devo, Bobbie, 105
Devo, Pud, 130
Devo, Spud, 130
Devo, Susan, 105

Diamond Dogs, 20
The Dictators, 61
Diddley, Bo, 36
Different Fur Studios, 76, 115
Disney, 151, 161
Dobb, J. R. "Bob," 35
Doctor Detroit, 137
Dolby, Thomas, 139
Donahue, Patty, 109
Dorsey, Lee, 134
Dove (rock band), 119
The Drome, 57
Dude magazine, 126
Duran Duran, 173
Duty Now For The Future, 117-119
Dylan, Bob, 19-20, 115

E

The Eagles, 11, 40-41
East Village, NY, 111
The Ed Sullivan Show, 14, 67
Eddie and the Hot Rods, 61
Edfred's, 99
Elfman, Danny, 131
Elias, Eddie, 4
Ellis, Jim, 159
Emerson, Lake & Palmer, 29
Enigma Records, 148-149
Eno, Brian, 75-76, 83-85, 86, 91
Erie Agricultural Fair, 3
The Eurythmics, 76, 173
E-Z Listening Disc, 148

F

Fazzin, Art, 8
The Feelies, 59
Fellini, Federico, 103
Fieger, Doug, 108
The Fifth Of July, 130
Firestone, 2, 100, 107

Firestone Country Club, 4
Firestone High School, 2, 49
Firestone Park, 2
Firestone, Rod, 52, 111
Fischer, Wild Man, 131
Fleetwood Mac, 11, 76
Fleming, Art, 8
Flintstone, Fred, 105
Flossy Bobbitt, 29
The F-Models, 109
Foghat, 42
Foreigner, 136
Fox network, 154
Fox Theatre, 169
Fox, Michael J., 102, 144
Fox, Mrs., 14
Freed, Alan, 1, 5-8
Freedom Of Choice (album), 123-128, 131
Freedom Of Choice (book), 41
Freese, Josh, 157, 169
Fridays (TV show), 125
Fripp, Robert, 75
Funicello, Annette, 17

G

Gable, Clark, 2
Garrett, Leif, 150
General Boy, 48, 169
General Tire, 2
The Generators, 102
The Germs, 72
Gertz, Jami, 138
Ginsberg, Allen, 49
Glass Harp, 103
The Go-Go's, 72
Gold, Andrew, 130
Gold, Dolli Quattrocchi, 136
Goodrich, 2, 100
Goodrich Junior High, 2
Goodyear, 2, 46, 51, 100
Goodyear Heights, 2

Goodyear World of Rubber, 47
Greenspan, Anita, 162
Gregg, Chris, 117
Gregg, Peter, 30
The Groundlings, 131
Gummi Savors, 153

H

Hager, Josh, 169
Haight-Ashbury, 16
Halle's, 31
Hamburg, New York, 3
Hammer Damage, 67, 111
Hammer, Mike, 52, 108
Hansen, Randy, 140
Hardcore, 167
Hardcore Devo, 168
Harrison, George, 63
Harry, Debbie, 61-62, 67, 130
Heaton, Michael, 41
Heavy Metal (film), 134
Heisman Trophy, 4
Heisman, John, 4
Hendrix, Jimi, 20, 140
Herbie: Fully Loaded, 154
Herman, Pee-wee, 131
Heroes, 76
Highland Square, 55, 91, 109, 110
Holiday Inn, 81
Hollywood, 25, 72, 102, 171
Hollywood Palladium, 72
Holmstrom, John, 61
Hopper, Dennis, 115
Houston, 137
Human Highway, 71, 113-115
Human Switchboard, 109
Hunter, Ian, 66
Hurricane Bob, 107
Hynde, Chrissie, 9, 15-16, 20, 23-24, 25-26, 30, 86, 107, 164, 175
Hynde, Terry, 30

I

I Want My MTV (book), 127, 135
Imij, Jimi, 110
The Immortal Porpoises, 35
Interior, Lux, 68, 110, 111
In The Beginning Was The End (book), 28
In The Beginning Was The End: The Truth About De-Evolution (film), 57, 69
Instagram, 10
The Island Of Dr. Moreau, 56
Island Records, 79
Ivy, Poison, 110

J

Jackett, Gary "General," 28, 37-38, 47
Jagger, Mick, 90
James (rock band), 159
James, LeBron, 9, 50, 101
The James Gang, 40, 103
Jarmusch, Jim, 111
Jazz & Pop magazine, 92
J.B.'s tavern, 48, 103, 106, 112
Jeopardy!, 8
Jett, Joan, 102
Jihad Jerry & The Evildoers, 161
The Jitters, 33
Jocko-Homo Heavenbound, 34-35
Joel, Billy, 62
John, Elton, 118
Jones, Marti, 107
Jones, Steve, 61
Journey, 136
Journey Covenant Church, 12
Jungle Jim, 37
Just A Gigolo (film), 75

K

Kamins, Mark, 109
Kansas City, MO, 8
Keenan, Devo, 159
Keenan, Maynard James, 159
Kendrick, David, 148
Kennedy, John F., 91, 133
Kent State University, 16-17, 22, 23-27, 29, 31-32, 35, 37, 40-41, 47, 162
Kent, Ohio, 16-17, 21, 31, 33, 41, 42, 45, 48, 103, 106, 112, 129, 174
Kerouac, Jack, 49
Kid Galahad, 8
Kidney, Robert, 36-37
King Cobra, 51-52
Kingston, Jamaica, 81
The Kinks, 2
Kiss (rock group), 120
Klaxons, 152
The Knack, 108
Knebworth Festival, 87-88
Knight, Bobby, 29
Kojak (TV show), 61
Korn, 159
The Kove, 37
Kraftwerk, 76, 97
KROQ (Los Angeles), 128

L

LA Forum, 152
LA Staff, 28
LA Weekly, 164-165
Lake Erie, 1
Lauper, Cyndi, 145
Leary, Timothy, 131, 139
Leary, Zachary, 139
Led Zeppelin, 148
The Lego Movie, 154
Lennon, John, 66
Lewis, Bob, 26-27, 29-30, 35, 97-98, 104-105, 109
Life magazine, 7

Light Of Day, 102
Little Rascals, 30
Little Richard, 37
Liverpool, 105
Lloyd, Christopher, 144
Locher, Ralph, 15
Lollapalooza, 158-159, 166
London, 86, 87, 107, 177
Long Beach, CA, 121
Los Angeles, 59, 68, 69-70, 72, 92, 95, 98, 126, 133, 136, 137, 139
Los Angeles Dodgers, 96
The Los Angeles Times, 171
Lost In Space, 151
Low, 76
Lowe, Nick, 91
Lowe's Theater, 164
Luigi's restaurant, 111
Lust For Life, 71, 83
Lynott, Phil, 107

M

Mabuhay Gardens, 71, 76
Mad World (book), 109
Madness, 92
Maerth, Oscar Kiss, 28, 35
Malibu, CA, 71
Man-Ray Studio, 35, 55, 57
Margouleff, Robert, 123-124
Marsh, David, 60, 119
Martin, Marilyn, 140-141
Mathis, Johnny, 19
Max's Kansas City, 66, 68, 75
McDonald's, 3, 47, 154, 160
MC5, 61
McFly, Marty, 144
McNeil, Legs, 61
The Measles, 31
Melody Maker, 76, 81, 86, 105
Menches, Charles, 3
Mercury Records, 105

Midnight Special (TV show), 92
The Mighty Morphin Power Rangers, 157
Mine Is Not A Holy War, 162
Minneapolis, 47
Mintz, Leo, 5-6
Mr. Jingeling, 31
Mr. Potato Head, 13
The Mr. Potato Head Show, 154
The Mods, 15
Moebius & Plank, 76
Mohawk Rubber, 2
Moondog Coronation Ball, 7
The Moondog Rock And Roll House Party, 7
Mosey, Jon, 52, 112
Mothersbaugh, Al, 144
Mothersbaugh, Alex, 118, 139
Mothersbaugh, Bob, 16, 33, 48, 118, 123, 139, 154, 158
Mothersbaugh, Jim, 16, 33, 48, 124
Mothersbaugh, Mark, 10, 11-17, 19-22, 26, 27, 29, 30-31, 32, 33, 35-36, 37, 39-41, 42, 45-46, 49-50, 52-53, 54, 55-56, 65-66, 71, 72, 80-82, 85, 87-88, 91-92, 93, 105, 15, 118, 124, 127, 128, 130, 131-133, 137, 143-145, 148-150, 151-153, 154-155, 157-160, 162, 166, 168, 171-172, 174, 175, 176-177
Mothersbaugh, Mary, 12, 169
Mothersbaugh, Robert Sr., 12, 48, 92, 98, 169
Mott The Hoople, 66
MTV, 91, 127, 135-136, 137, 139, 147, 176
Mullens, Ron "Pete Sake," 52
Mumi, Bill, 151
Muni, Scott, 8
Murdoch Company, 46

Music For Insomniacs, 144, 154
Musarra, Russ, 99
Mutato Muzika, 151-152
Muzak, 148
Myers, Alan, 48-49, 143, 148, 167
Myers, Richard, 47

N

Nagy, Evie, 41
Nancy (comic book), 120
National Football League, 4
Nelson, Rick, 28
New Musical Express, 81, 128
New Orleans, 134
New Traditionalists, 131-135
New Wave Nigel, 160
New York City, 7-8, 40, 59, 65-67, 68, 72, 75, 83, 96, 103, 109, 110, 145, 155
The New York Dolls, 60, 66
New York Rocker, 96, 105
The New York Times, 152-153
New York Yankees, 96
Newman, Laraine, 130-131
Newsday, 124
Nicholis, Nick, 67, 102-105
Nicks, Stevie, 141
Niemeyer, Oscar, 152
Nike, 154
Nine Inch Nails, 161
Nixon, Richard, 23
Nomi, Klaus, 103
North Hollywood, CA, 117
The Numbers Band (15-60-75), 30, 31, 36-37

O

Oakland, CA, 169
Ocasek, Ric, 97
Oh, No! It's Devo, 136
Ohio & Erie Canal, 1
Ohio River, 1

The Ohio State University, 23
Ohio University, 23
Oingo Boingo, 131
O'Neil's, 79, 99
Orr, Benjamin, 97
Ostin, Mo, 132

P

Packard Gallery, 41
The Pagans, 57
Paramount Theater, 7
Parker, Sarah Jessica, 137-138
Peabody's Down Under, 149
Pee-wee's Big Adventure, 131
Pee-wee's Playhouse, 144-145
Pere Ubu, 52, 57, 60, 105
Peter Gunn, 8
Tom Petty and Heartbreakers, 52, 97, 135, 141
Phaedrus, 125
Philadelphia, 68
Piccadilly Inn, 52
Pink Flamingos, 37
Pink Floyd, 11, 59
Pirate's Cove, 53
The Police, 144
Polsky's, 99
The Poor Girls, 127
Pop, Iggy, 60, 70-71, 83
Popular Science magazine, 45
Portage Hotel, 3, 101
Powell, Mike, 29
Power Station studio, 133
Pray TV, 119
Presley, Elvis, 8, 19, 97, 148
The Pretty Things, 110
Professional Bowlers Association, 4
Punk magazine, 61
The Punks (rock band), 60
Purkhiser, Erick, 110
Purkhiser, Mike, 111

Q

Q: Are We Not Men? We Are Devo!, 89-93, 97, 119
Quaker Oats, 101
Quaker Square Mall, 46
Queen, 20, 136
Queen City Records, 55
Question Mark & The Mysterians, 61
Quinn, Martha, 136

R

Ra, Sun, 17, 43
Radio Shack, 49
The Ramones, 40, 61, 62
Rancid, Vince, 110
Raspberries, 15, 103
The Rathskeller, 42, 103
Rauschenberg, Robert, 45
Reagan, Ronald, 133
Reckless: My Life As A Pretender, 9
Record Plant (Los Angeles), 123-124, 133, 139
Record Rendezvous, 7
Reiner, Rob, 150
Reisman, Rod, 31-32
Request Review, 5
Reubens, Paul, 131, 144-145
Rhodes, James, 24-25
Riverside, CA, 129-130
Roberts, Elliot, 95
Robinson Memorial Hospital, 57
Robinson, Dave, 79-80, 85, 107
Robinson, Will, 151
Rock and Roll Hall of Fame, 1, 171-173
Rockefeller, John D., 53
Rocket From The Tombs, 60
Rocket Power, 160
Rockne, Knute, 4
Rodriguez, Chi Chi, 89
Rollerball, 118

Rolling Stone magazine, 11, 91, 92, 95, 118, 137, 148
The Rolling Stones, 19, 20, 57, 89-90, 96, 110
Rooter, Donut, 130-131
Rooter, Rod, 131
Rorschach test, 161
Rothwell, Craig Allen, 92
Rotten, Johnny, 77, 81-82
Roxy Music, 20
The Royal Tenenbaums, 154
Rubber Ball gala, 2
Rubber Bowl, 2
Rubber Capital of the World, 2
Rubber City Rebels, 52, 103, 108, 111
Rubber Room nightclub, 2-3
Ruby & The Romantics, 8
Rudman, Kal, 125
Rugrats, 154
Rundgren, Todd, 95
Rushmore, 154

S

St. Louis, 8
Saint Patrick's Elementary School, 120
Salem, Ohio, 5
San Francisco, 16, 71, 72, 76, 113, 115, 169
San Clemente, CA, 28
Santa Monica, CA, 127
Sat Sun Mat, 15
Satrom, LeRoy, 24
Saturday Night Live, 73, 95-96, 117, 119, 125, 130, 154
Schmidt, Sue, 128
Schrader, Paul, 102
Schwartz, Michael W., 131
Scott, Ken, 117-118
SDS, 21, 32

Search And Destroy magazine, 77
Seiberling, 2, 100
The Sex Pistols, 61, 77
Sextet Devo, 31
Shout, 139-140, 143
Silver Apples, 17
Simmons, Silvie, 107
Sinatra, Frank, 7, 17, 19
Sire Records, 62, 108
Sirius radio, 162
Slaughterhouse Rock, 148
Sluggo, 120
Smith, Debbie, 107, 127
Smooth Noodle Maps, 149
Snoop Dogg, 159
Soap Box Derby, 4
Something For Everybody, 165
Somewhere In England, 63
Sounds magazine, 81, 106
Sparks, 148
Spazz Attack, 92, 137
Speed Racer, 152
Spinal Tap, 155
The Spirit Of '76, 150
Spitz-Kalmus, Shaylah, 127
Springsteen, Bruce, 95
Spungen, Nancy, 77
Square Pegs, 138
Stardust, Ziggy, 20, 75
Starr, Ringo, 14
Starwood nightclub, 69-70, 72, 95
State Road Shopping Center, 92
Statler, Chuck, 45, 47, 91
Stein, Chris, 67
Stein, Seymour 62
Sternberg, Liam, 80, 107
Stiff Records, 49, 79, 85, 86, 106-107
Stockwell, Dean, 113, 115
The Stooges, 77
Summers, Andy, 144
Summit Beach Park, 4

Summit Mall, 17
The Sundance Film Festival, 157
Sunset Strip, 69, 152
Supercop, 161
Superman, 103
Supertramp, 118
Sweet, Rachel, 85, 107
Swingos, 70

T

Talking Heads, 62
Tank Girl, 157
Teenage Jesus And The Jerks, 59
Temple, Julien, 83
Tepperman, Muffy, 138
Thin Lizzy, 107
Thomas, David, 57
Thorpe, Jim, 4
Johnny Thunders and the Heartbreakers, 52
Time magazine, 24-25
Tin Huey, 30, 70, 101, 104, 106, 108, 109
Tokyo, 76
Total Devo, 148
Toyota, 149
Trans, 115
Travolta, John, 42
Tricky, 159
The Troggs, 8
Trouser Press, 105
Tsin San Buddhist monastery, 28
The Tubes, 68, 69
21 Jump Street, 154
The Twist-Offs, 144

U

Ullman, Tracey, 107
Ultravox, 76
Unit 5, 109
Unit Services Shop, 46
United Rubber Workers, 3

Universal Amphitheatre, 137
University of Akron, 32, 103, 107
University of Indiana, 30
US Festival, 62
U2, 62

V
Van Halen, 135
Vancouver, 166
The Vandals, 144
Velvet Underground, 20, 59, 105
Vicious, Sid, 77
Vietnam War, 19, 20, 23, 62
Village Voice, 92, 104-105
Virgin Records, 79-80, 85-87

W
The Waitresses, 30, 109
WAKR (Akron), 5, 8
Wallace, Kristy, 110
Walsh, Joe, 21, 30, 31, 40-41, 129, 141, 162
Walt Disney Records, 161
Warhol, Andy, 20, 45
Warner Brothers Records, 79, 85-87, 89-90, 91, 106, 108, 119, 123, 125-126, 131-132, 140, 147-148
Warner, Brad, 99-101, 110-111
The Washington Post, 59
Waters, John, 37, 169
Watson, Bobbie, 35, 65
Wayne's World, 90
Weber, Fred, 31-32, 33
Welch, Ward, 52
Wells, H.G., 56
Wenner, Jann, 91
We're All Devo (video), 131
West Hollywood, CA, 152
Whisky a Go-Go, 72, 152

White Nights, 141
The White Stripes, 168
WHK Auditorium, 43
The Who, 20
Winkler, Scott, 108
WINS (New York), 7-8
Winter Olympics, 166
Winter, Johnny, 130
Winterland Ballroom, 77
Wipeouters, 160
WJW (Cleveland), 5
WMMS (Cleveland), 43, 97
Wonder Woman (comic book), 35
Wonder, Stevie, 124
Wood, Ron, 95
Woodridge High School, 16
Woodstock, NY, 108
Word Of Mouth, 130
World Series of Golf, 4
World War II, 12, 19
Wyman, Bill, 19
WZIP (Akron), 103

X

Y
Yardbirds, 119, 162
Yes, 29
Young, Neil, 71, 96, 113-115

Z
Zappa, Frank, 41, 49, 119
Zero Defex, 110
Zevon, Warren, 130
ZZ Top, 135

▶ PHOTO CREDITS

Cover photo – DMI/The LIFE Picture Collection
Page 3 – Library of Congress Prints and Photographs Division Washington, D.C. 20540.
Page 6 – Author's collection.
Page 9 – Courtesy of John Mascolo.
Page 34 – Author's collection.
Page 36 – Author's collection.
Page 46 – Author's collection.
Page 49 – Author's collection.
Page 53 – Author's collection.
Page 56 – Author's collection.
Page 80 – kathclick / BigStockPhoto.com.
Page 81 – s_bukley / BigStockPhoto.com.
Page 90 – Denis Makarenko / BigStockPhoto.com.
Page 100 – Author's collection.
Page 102 – Author's collection.
Page 104 – Author's collection.
Page 106 – newsfocus1 / BigStockPhoto.com.
Page 114 – DFree / BigStockPhoto.com.
Page 126 – Author's collection.
Page 153 – s_bukley / BigStockPhoto.com.
Page 158 – Author's collection.
Page 163 – s_bukley / BigStockPhoto.com.
Page 164 – Author's collection.
Page 166 – Author's collection.
Page 168 – Author's collection.
Page 172 – Author's collection.
Page 176 – kathclick / BigStockPhoto.com.

I owe a debt of gratitude to following individuals: John Mascolo, Mary Ellen Huesken, Mike Olszewski, Jon Mosey, Terry Hynde, Robert Kidney, Harvey Gold, Dolli Quattrocchi Gold and Danny Basone.

Lastly, to all the Akronites reading this book: Growing up in the Rubber City, there was nothing better than standing on the devil's strip while listening to Howie and snacking on some jojo's and sauerkraut balls.

www.ingramcontent.com/pod-product-compliance
Lightning Source LLC
Chambersburg PA
CBHW050029090426
42735CB00021B/3424